Download the New  app:

- get early access to every issue
- follow every move on the built-in board

Read New In Chess on your tablet, smartphone or Windows PC, two weeks before the printed edition is available, and replay all the moves in the interactive chess viewer

You can now download the digital edition of New In Chess on your tablet, phone or PC/notebook and read all the stories immediately after publication. By simply tapping on the games you can replay the moves on the interactive chessviewer. So from now on you don't need a board and set to fully enjoy what top grandmasters have to say about their games! The New In Chess app installs in seconds, has all the right features and is easy to operate. We have made an entire issue available as a FREE DOWNLOAD.

The chess magazine that moves
Now available for iOS, Android and Windows

NEW IN CHESS bestsellers

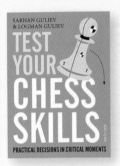

Test Your Chess Skills
Practical Decisions in Critical Moments
Sarhan & Logman Guliev   180 pages - €19.95

The test positions, unknown outside the former Soviet Union, cover the entire spectrum of what a modern club player should know. Find tactical blows, deep strategic manoeuvres, opening traps, standard endgame plans and other principles in action. Each solution of the 224 tests is a detailed, practical and to-the-point lesson, always offering a helpful general conclusion.

The Full English Opening
Mastering the Fundamentals
Carsten Hansen   464 pages - €29.95

The first one-volume book that covers all variations.

"Currently the best guide in the market. Hansen has clearly put in an amazing amount of work into this book." *IM Kevin Goh Wein Ming*

"A thorough grounding, where the subtleties of the move orders are carefully weighed up, as are the various counters by Black." – *GM Glenn Flear, Yearbook*

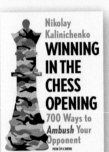

Winning in the Chess Opening
700 Ways to Ambush Your Opponent
Nikolay Kalinichenko   464 pages - €24.95

More than just a collection of traps and tricks. Kalinichenko always explains the ideas and plans behind the opening and how play could have been improved.

"Enjoyable, while also making the reader much more aware of where early pitfalls can suddenly spring from." *CHESS Magazine*

Clinch it!
How to Convert an Advantage into a Win in Chess
Cyrus Lakdawala   256 pages - €27.95

IM Lakdawala has identified dozens of reasons why we see wins turn into draws or even losses. Learn how to efficiently exploit a development lead, capitalize on an attack, identify and convert favourable imbalances, accumulate strategic advantages. With compelling examples and captivating and often funny explanations.

"Packed full of common sense and should help to improve your conversion rate." – *CHESS Magazine (UK)*

Strategic Chess Exercises
Find the Right Way to Outplay Your Opponent
Emmanuel Bricard   224 pages - €24.95

Finally an exercises book that is not about tactics!

"Bricard is clearly a very gifted trainer. He selected a superb range of positions and explains the solutions extremely well." – *Grandmaster Daniel King*

"For chess coaches this book is nothing short of phenomenal." – *Carsten Hansen, author of The Full English Opening*

Play 1...d6 Against Everything
A Compact and Ready-to-use Black Repertoire for Club Players
Erik Zude & Jörg Hickl   208 pages - €22.95

Develop your position with strong standard moves and start effective counterplay. Zude and Hickl explain all typical characteristics and give practical examples.
"Very useful for club players and casual players looking for a well-explained and complete opening repertoire."
Uwe Bekemann, German Correspondence Chess

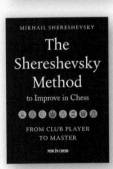

The Shereshevsky Method to Improve in Chess
From Club Player to Master
Mikhail Shereshevsky   352 pages - €27.95

"A must for all chess trainers and chess players who wish to improve their performance, because it covers all the skills a good chess player needs." – *International Master Dirk Schuh*

"New In Chess scored a bit of a coup getting this book." *Mark Crowther, editor of The Week In Chess*

"Well done, New In Chess! Now sign up the author for another book, as soon as possible." – *Sean Marsh, CHESS Magazine*

Dismantling the Sicilian
A Complete Modern Repertoire for White
Jesus de la Villa & Max Illingworth   368 pages - €27.95

"Many novelties and improvements on existing theory have been added."
Carsten Hansen, author of The Chameleon Sicilian

"Novelties abound. A high-quality and durable repertoire that has the potential to cause significant theoretical and practical problems." – *Paul Hopwood, CHESS Magazine*

"A total knockout." – *ChessVibes*

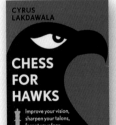

Chess for Hawks
Improve your vision, sharpen your talons, forget your fear
Cyrus Lakpdawala   288 pages - €22.95

WINNER: Best Instructional Book
Chess Journalists of America

"A very good manual for those who feel they got stuck at a certain level and can't quite find the way to break through to the next level."
Carsten Hansen, author of 'The Chameleon Variation'

The Art of the Tarrasch Defence
Strategies, Techniques and Surprising Ideas
Alexey Bezgodov   320 pages - €27.95

"A goldmine of resource (...) brilliantly written."
Michael Mkpadi, ChessHot

"Well suited for all levels of player, but particularly those around 1800-2200, who are looking to learn how classical chess is played." – *IM John Donaldson*

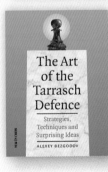

available at your local (chess)bookseller or at www.newinchess.com

2019#2
NEW ♟ IN CHESS

2

Contents

'Your chess style represents your personality'

CONTRIBUTORS TO THIS ISSUE
Erwin l'Ami, Vishy Anand, Vladislav Artemiev, Adhiban Baskaran, Jeroen Bosch, Maxim Dlugy, Andrey Esipenko, Jorden van Foreest, Anish Giri, Vidit Gujrathi, John Henderson, Murali Karthikeyan, Peter Heine Nielsen, Maxim Notkin, Arthur van de Oudeweetering, Judit Polgar, Teimour Radjabov, Matthew Sadler, Jan Timman

Go, Lasker!

This photo – dated '7 March, 1930' – shows Emanuel Lasker being the 'game changer', as the second World Champion turns his strategic mindset from chess to the ancient Chinese game of Go, to challenge Germany's Felix Dueball, one of the world's leading Go players at the time.

Perhaps Lasker was ahead of the curve, as this certainly wasn't the last time there's been a crossover between the two strategic games. The critically acclaimed 2017 documentary about Google DeepMind's 'AlphaGo' was said by Magnus Carlsen's coach, Peter Heine Nielsen, to be 'The best chess movie he'd ever seen,' as it explains the groundbreaking AI work from DeepMind CEO Demis Hassabis and his team, as they make the crossover – though in reverse – by first conquering Go, and now onto chess, with AlphaZero.

Lasker was a unique figure, whose intellectual horizon and ambitions went far beyond chess. This rare photo of Lasker playing Go will be published in *Emanuel Lasker Volume II: Games & Psychology – Beyond the Limits of Chess*, the follow-up to the acclaimed first volume of the Lasker trilogy (enthusiastically reviewed by Matthew Sadler in New In Chess 2018/8), expected late 2019. ∎

Chess Park Tavern

It's never easy when we hear of a once popular public chess park being closed due to the redevelopment of an area. One such is located in an alley off Brand Boulevard in Glendale in Los Angeles, with the removal of its beautifully designed 16 concrete chess tables, to make way for a wooden deck that will be used for outside seating and live entertainment for a new bar and restaurant.

Of course, city officials and developers see this as a way of breathing new life into the space. Some developers perhaps might not care for a location's past history or heritage; on the other hand, some developers do care, and they may well try and blend in by maintaining the theme – and that's just what happened with the new Chess Park Tavern that's set to open its doors in early March after reaching a five-year agreement with the city to take over the space.

When it opened in 2004, the chess park was bustling with players, explained tavern spokesman Arthur Mkrtchyan to the *Los Angeles Times*, adding that in the intervening years activity in the space simply dropped off. But while the chess tables are gone, Mkrtchyan isn't throwing away all the pieces of the past, as he plans to host tavern chess nights once or twice a month to keep the 'chess vibes' going.

The tavern is also providing boards and chess pieces to players, and those monthly events could include tournaments with prize money. Not only

The new Chess Park Tavern doesn't betray its past.

that, but the tavern's cups will have chess-piece handles and the design team is working on producing chess-piece inspired lights to replace the five street lights that were removed for the deck's construction, to keep in with the aesthetics of its past history.

Cover girl

A quick trivia question: Which American was the first chessplayer to appear on the cover of *Sports Illustrated* magazine? Be honest now, how many of you answered Bobby Fischer? Well, not only the wrong player, but also the wrong sex! The answer is Lisa Lane, the two-time U.S. Women's Champion, who appeared on the cover of the August 7, 1961 edition of *SI* – years before Fischer achieved this feat en route to becoming World Champion.

That original feature on Lane (by Robert Cantwell, entitled 'Queen of Knights and Pawns'), was revisited recently by staff writer Emma Baccellieri in the December 17, 2018 edition of *SI*, with another article on how equality still eludes women in chess even more than five decades after her groundbreaking appearance.

Jimmy Adams penned an interesting profile of chess diva Lane in New In Chess 2012/2, and how she made newspaper headlines after withdrawing from the 1961/62 Hastings tournament because she was too much in love to concentrate on her games. Due to a lack of funding back then from the US Chess Federation, Lane became disillusioned with the chess scene and hung up her pawns, and instead turned to running a natural health food business in the small upstate New York town of Carmel.

A couple of years ago, Lane sold her own personal copy (autographed) of that groundbreaking *SI* magazine from 1961 on eBay. She's retired now, though still living in Carmel, and although aged 80, still very sharp if our telephone conversation with her

was anything to go by! She explained that apart from a short bio, she simply wrote in the ad: 'This magazine is from my personal collection. I signed

Lisa Lane's personal signed copy of a memorable Sports Illustrated edition.

the cover with a Blue Sharpie. I was the first of only two chess players ever to appear on the cover of *Sports Illustrated*. The other chess player was my friend Bobby Fischer in 1972.' Perhaps as a sad reflection of our times, she only received $30 from the auction...

Chess Hotel

The greatest chess player of the 18th century was unquestionably François-André Danican Philidor (1726-1795). However, his main source of income was music, and he is recognized as one of the most popular pre-revolutionary French composers of his day. A bust of recognition of the great man can be found carved on the side of the Paris Opera House.

And nearby, we've discovered a new chic and arty Paris chess-themed hotel slap bang in the middle of said Opera district. The Chess Hotel (thechesshotel.com) features a chess board-themed aesthetic and original design, conceived by the internationally renowned interior architecture partnership of Patrick Gilles and Dorothée Boissier, where the talented

Brushing your teeth at the Chess Hotel. Who doesn't want a bathroom like this?

duo showcase high-quality materials – linen, oak, Carrara marble – with their unique glimpse into the world of Chess. Many other artists have also contributed to creating its unique decoration, including Pierre-Elie de Pibrac with his photos of the Opera de Paris, one of which shows – whether by accident or design – Philidor's bust!

The four-star hotel describes itself as: 'A place away from the hustle and bustle of the city, it invites travellers to enjoy a game of chess by the fire, a glass of champagne in its bar or a quiet evening in one of its elegant rooms.' To enjoy a game or two in the convivial surroundings, throughout you'll find strategically-placed wooden French Lardy Chess Sets and boards.

And whilst we're in Paris

Every so often or not, FIDE tries to slide chess into the Olympic Games – but their latest attempt did come with a sense of poignant history attached to it, with the launching of a campaign by new FIDE president Arkady Dvorkovich for chess to be included in the 2024 Paris Olympics.

The International Olympic Committee (IOC) recognized chess as a sport back in 1999, and the signs looked promising for a possible inclusion when Vishy Anand and Alexei Shirov took part in a demonstration event at the Sydney Olympics the following year. But since then, the IOC has failed to include chess.

However, Dvorkovich persevered, and in conjunction with the French Chess Federation, embarked on a high-profile social media/media campaign to lobby for the inclusion of chess to become an additional or demonstration sport for the Paris 2024 Olympic Games – alas, to no avail, as chess lost out again, to – of all things – breakdancing!

A pity really, as there was a lot of symbolic history here. The Paris 2024 Olympics not only celebrates the centenary of the 1924 Paris Olympics, it is also the centenary of FIDE, formed that same year in Paris during the peak of Olympic

Arkady Dvorkovich playing Sophie Milliet at the launch of a new Olympic FIDE campaign. It's not too late to learn breakdancing, is it?

fervour in the city. To commemorate their creation, FIDE organized the first world amateur championship as a side event to the Paris Olympics, described as the 'Tournoi Olympique', won by Latvian master Herman Mattison, ahead of Edgar Colle and Max Euwe.

Spirit of the game

It's not often we go digging up news for NIC's Café by reading prominent archaeology magazines and websites, such as *Archaeology Today*, *British Archaeology* and *Smithsonian* – but recently they all featured a 'spirited' chess-related story. It all centres around two 19th century chess pieces that were discovered hidden in a barn.

The two pieces, a queen and a bishop, which date from around 1850, were surreptitiously tucked away in a wooden beam in the barn, which is located in the sleepy rural English town of Burgh le Marsh, Lincolnshire. There, over the entrance, the little figurines stayed, unnoticed, for some 170 years. But when the new owner of the property decided to renovate the barn, the chess pieces were discovered. And immediately it begs the question: why put them there in the first place?

Archaeologist Dr Adam Daubney, from Lincolnshire City Council, provided the answer: 'We know that in the 1800s, people used to place artefacts at boundaries and thresholds of properties to help ward off evil spirits. These tended to be like shoes, miniature bibles or mummified cats. We haven't seen chess pieces before. The pieces were found in the beam which was over the main access point of the barn, so I think these have been purposely selected and placed to help keep the occupiers and their livestock safe. It seems likely that the praying Bishop and Queen – the latter of which might have served the role of Mary – were carefully selected from

For 170 years this Queen and praying Bishop warded off evil spirits in Burgh le Marsh.

the chess set as pieces that might have particular spiritual power to ward off evil.' Think of that when you next play your queen or one of your bishops! ∎

Gaping abyss

I just received the latest copy of New In Chess (2019/1) and spotted an omission. Well it is more of a gaping abyss than a large omission actually. I am unable to find Nigel Short's column 'Short Stories'. This is a rather egregious start to my New Year. I trust that this was a mere blip and that my erstwhile English countryman will be back for the next issue – after all his column is chiefly the reason that I subscribe to the magazine – and it is the very first piece that I turn to each time.

Carl Portman
Banbury, England

Why?

I enjoy a lot the articles of GM Nigel Short. Please let me know why his column didn't appear in New In Chess 2019/1?

Guy J. Bendana
Miami, FL, USA

Refreshingly straightforward

My New In Chess 2019/1 arrived today. As usual, I turned first (or, more accurately, tried to turn first) to my favourite feature of your estimable publication: Short Stories. Imagine my surprise (and vexation) when Nigel's wit and wisdom (or, rarely, nonsense) was nowhere to be found. Please tell me that this omission was a one-time event. I find GM Short's column to be interesting, well written, and (last but not least) refreshingly straightforward in its treatment of whatever aspect of the chess world the GM chooses to discuss. I will sorely miss it (and would appreciate a full explanation) if Short Stories has been discontinued.

Ken Marshall
Lombard, IL, USA

The best columnist

It is with deep disappointment that I have learned that Nigel Short will no longer publish his columns in New In Chess. You should know that his columns were the only reason why I kept on purchasing New In Chess. In my modest opinion, Nigel is the best columnist in the chess world.

I sincerely hope that you will reconsider your decision.

Denis-Emmanuel Philippe
Brussels, Belgium

Editorial postscript

Just like many of our readers, we are (obviously) big fans of Nigel Short's writings. But it is true that we decided to discontinue his column. The reason is that we feel Nigel Short's new position as FIDE vice-president conflicts with what we expect a columnist to be: an independent voice who can say whatever he wants. We feel that his political position would inevitably restrict him. The decision has certainly nothing to do with the quality of his work. Not at all. That's why we have asked Nigel Short to keep writing for us and we very much hope he will. Nigel is a wonderful chess writer and we are confident we will have many more great pieces by him in New In Chess.

'Unique' personality

I was looking forward to reading an in-depth background piece on Samuel Reshevsky in New In Chess 2019/1, and was dismayed to see what a one-sided hatchet job it was. Literally nothing good to say of a man with an impressive 'stands on its own' record in chess, who grew up under horrible circumstances and who lived a life outside of chess as well.

A very poor job by the editor to allow such an overwhelmingly negative article to be published in a preeminent chess magazine. One of the low points for me was when the author described Reshevsky's face as looking like a rat. There were several

other descriptions in the article that were as bad.

There are numerous other famous chess players with 'unique' personalities, but I have never seen anyone go after them with such unmitigated vehemence. As for the repeated comments concerning Reshevsky's will to win, I'd believe all top chess players must possess this trait to get to the top, to be relentless and driven. A better question might be, which ones do not?

I expect New In Chess to have better standards than this.

Jeff Taylor
Annandale, VA, USA

Gossip and hokey theories

I was surprised by the critical nature of the article on Sammy Reshevsky, one of the strongest players of the twentieth century, in New In Chess 2019/1. Admittedly, if one wishes to critique a famous player's personal qualities (always a judgmental and self-righteous undertaking) there is no lack of material.

You could easily choose someone like Alekhine, a purported drunk and chessboard coward running from his strongest challenger. Another choice might be Fischer who, unlike Morphy, and purportedly Steinitz, didn't wait until later in life before going mad and whose antics drove organizers, and by design his opponents, to distraction and frustration. There is also Tal, the reported drug and alcohol addict, and there are obviously many others.

However, many chess players are more interested in the games played by these chess geniuses, their ideas and grand conceptions presented over the board and it is this quality of famous players that I prefer to read about in New In Chess. Gossip and hokey theories? Not so much interested.

Was Reshevsky really a lumberjack at the chessboard, with questionable strategic ability, whose play was inaccurate and unrefined? One

wonders why the Soviets feared him and resorted to conspiring against him in the 1953 Candidates tournament. Jeff Sonas has him ranked as #1 in the world for 14 different months between 1942 and 1953. How did he

---

Write to us

New In Chess, P.O. Box 1093
1810 KB Alkmaar, The Netherlands
or e-mail: editors@newinchess.com
Letters may be edited or abridged

---

rise to be at or near the top of the chess world for so long and gain wins over Lasker, Capablanca, Alekhine, Euwe, Botvinnik, Smyslov and Fischer if he had questionable strategic understanding and was inaccurate and unrefined in his play? Just lucky perhaps?

Suppose I accept that Reshevsky was a second-rate strategist and a lumberjack of a player who lacked creativity, based on the author's argument, in part, that he had no openings or variations named after him. Should I instead enjoy the games of those creative, strategic and refined chess geniuses who do, such as Janos Balogh who invented the Balogh Defense (1.e4 d6 2.d4 f5) or Herman Clemenz, the creative genius behind the Clemenz Opening (1.h3) or Robert Durkin and his 1.♘a3 attack? Fortunately, as the author revealed, we have this yardstick to help us sort out the great players from the not so great.

Richard Bowes
Salt Springs, NB, Canada

Big Mac chess

I read with horror Max Dlugy's blasphemous article entitled 'Speeding Up' in your last edition, New In Chess 2019/1. His ideas of reducing proper chess to a race against the clock, golf to pitch and putt, snooker to pool and test cricket to a 20/20 lottery is just typical of this modern-day need for instant gratification instead of something more lasting and meaningful.

No doubt Max prefers a Big Mac to a chateaubriand and a quickie on the sofa to an evening of romance and tantalising seduction.

Max tries to justify his claims for pot noodle chess with some wishful notion that it would attract more participants and sponsors when in reality all it would do is drive anyone over forty out of the game and anyone younger with an IQ higher than a toilet brush to take up something like Go which could hardly be played properly at breakneck speed. Why do we need more sponsors anyway? Chess would be fine as just an amateur game, as for most of us it is, there is no need to commercialise it further or to make it popular with the type of brainless twits that now watch reality TV or listen to rap music.

I suppose that I should not be surprised by the nonsense spouted by Mister Dlugy, I guess it is the inevitable result of spending too long in the USA. No doubt he voted for Trump too.

Peter Cafolla
Kilcullen, Ireland

COLOPHON

PUBLISHER: Allard Hoogland
EDITOR-IN-CHIEF:
Dirk Jan ten Geuzendam
HONORARY EDITOR: Jan Timman
CONTRIBUTING EDITOR: Anish Giri
EDITORS: Peter Boel, René Olthof
PRODUCTION: Joop de Groot
TRANSLATORS: Ken Neat, Piet Verhagen
SALES AND ADVERTISING: Remmelt Otten

PHOTOS AND ILLUSTRATIONS IN THIS ISSUE:
Alina l'Ami, Maria Emelianova, David Llada,
Rosa de las Nieves, Lennart Ootes, Niki
Riga, Rudy Sakdalam, John Saunders

COVER PHOTO: New In Chess

© No part of this magazine may be reproduced,
stored in a retrieval system or transmitted in any
form or by any means, recording or otherwise,
without the prior permission of the publisher.

NEW IN CHESS
P.O. BOX 1093
1810 KB ALKMAAR
THE NETHERLANDS

PHONE: 00-31-(0)72-51 27 137
SUBSCRIPTIONS: nic@newinchess.com
EDITORS: editors@newinchess.com
ADVERTISING: otten@newinchess.com

WWW.NEWINCHESS.COM

Magnus Carlsen seals seventh victory in Wijk aan Zee

World Champion shakes off Anish Giri's challenge

Theo Henrar, Chairman of the Management Board of Tata Steel Nederland, hands Magnus Carlsen his seventh trophy. Anish Giri knows he has to wait for at least another year.

Ever since his stunning debut way back in 2004, when as a 13-year-old kid he made his first GM norm, Magnus Carlsen has had warm ties with Wijk aan Zee, where he won his first Masters four years later. At the end of the 81st Tata Steel tournament, the Norwegian phenomenon lifted the winner's trophy for a record seventh time, just like last year after a riveting duel with Anish Giri. **DIRK JAN TEN GEUZENDAM** reports from the Dutch North Sea coast.

As the 81st Tata Steel tournament was about to get under way, last year's jubilee edition had not yet been forgotten. Wouldn't it be wonderful if we saw another neck-and-neck race between Magnus Carlsen and local favourite Anish Giri? Last time, the World Champion had prevailed in a blitz play-off... would this edition bring the Dutchman's first victory in an elite event?

Of course not everyone was thinking like this, but in the previews it was an often-heard story. Nor did the players themselves dismiss the idea. When he drew number 7 at the opening ceremony, Giri didn't express relief with the extra white game, but instead immediately looked at the schedule and said with a satisfied smile that he would be White against Carlsen – in the final round.

The Norwegian had drawn number 14 and showed great composure – and foresight – when he calmly commented – with a reference to Dutch football legend Johan Cruyff – that 14 was not such a bad number to have in the Netherlands. But he, too, was ready for a race against Giri. After the first few rounds, he kept talking in his post-game interviews about his opponents as if they had been Giri, much to the bewilderment of many viewers. This typical Carlsen humour was not entirely appreciated by the organizers, who asked him to stop this and even had the 'Giri passages' edited out of the videos; not because they thought they were not funny, but because they feared it showed a lack of respect for the opponents Carlsen had really played against.

False start

Everyone was ready for two weeks of enticing rivalry, but then, before the rivals had even had a chance to warm up, Giri lost his first game, as White. Surprised by Ian Nepomniachtchi's choice of the Pirc, Giri mixed up various plans, undermined his own

position and lost in a mere 26 moves. For a moment, the dream scenario was out of the window, but the next day the Dutchman revived the hopes of his fans by beating Vladimir Kramnik with the black pieces.

Kramnik's performance in Wijk aan Zee could only be fully understood later, when it became clear that this had been his last serious tournament (see the interview on page 42). Till that moment, his risky, at times extravagant games had mainly been seen as a sequel to the dare-devil,

'Everyone was ready for two weeks of enticing rivalry between Carlsen and Giri.'

over-optimistic chess he had been playing of late. His loss against Giri was the first of six. After his final-round defeat against Sam Shankland he even ended up in shared last place. It was that game that, more than any other one, showed that the former World Champion was battling with an irresistible force. In a position in which he had a forced draw, he side-stepped that draw even though he had no winning chances at all and he had seen that he could get at best a draw and that a loss would be the more likely outcome.

NOTES BY
Anish Giri

Vladimir Kramnik
Anish Giri
Wijk aan Zee 2019 (2)
English Opening, Four Knights System

After the tournament Vladimir Kramnik shockingly announced his retirement, so this may very well have been my last classical game against

him. I was very fortunate to have won it, but one thing I can guarantee you: if Vladimir decides to publish a collection of his best games, he will (or should) include all seven consecutive wins he inflicted on me.

1.c4 e5 2.♘c3 ♘f6 3.♘f3 ♘c6 4.d3

Since I had discussed many different lines with Vladimir before the Candidates tournament in Berlin last year, where my role was to help him, this didn't come as a surprise. Yet I have the feeling I didn't react in the ideal fashion and overall I wasn't satisfied with how the opening went.

4...d5 5.cxd5 ♘xd5 6.e4

6.e3 was more the direction I was counting on, as Vladimir chose this against Karjakin in a rapid game last year.

6...♘xc3 It was also possible to withdraw the knight, as many of my colleagues have done.

7.bxc3

This structure usually occurs with colours reversed in some Sicilians. White's position here is pretty easy to play, and I knew Vladimir liked it.

7...♗c5 8.♗e2 0-0 9.0-0

9...♗b6 I don't like this move very much, but it isn't so bad. I am now, for example, ready to meet ♘d2 with ...♘a5, preparing the ...c7-c5 advance. 9...♕e7 was what I had briefly looked at, but during the game I had a blind spot and didn't understand why 10.d4?! wasn't possible: 10...exd4 11.cxd4 ♘xd4 12.♘xd4 ♖d8 13.♗b2 ♗xd4 14.♗xd4. And here, for some reason, I missed the brutal 14...♕xe4!. Sure, White could have played something else on move 10, but then I am not sure I would actually have committed myself to ...♗b6.

10.a4 ♖e8 11.♕c2 ♕f6

I was aiming for the g6-square, as in the fashionable ♕f3-♕g3 variation of the Taimanov with colours reversed, but in hindsight it was better to have gone via d6.

12.♔h1!? A not very subtle hint that the f-pawn will advance sooner rather than later.

12...h6?! I was ready to meet ♘d2 with ...♘a5, and I didn't really believe in the move Big Vlad actually made. I was worried that the immediate 12...♘a5!? would be met by 13.d4!?, but after 13...exd4, despite my pieces looking a bit uncoordinated, the

position is unclear, since Black will challenge White's pawn centre with ideas like ...♘c6, ...♗g4, etc.

13.♘g1!? 13.♘e1!? was actually also a serious candidate.

13...♕d6 A bit desperate. I correctly judged that 13...g5 was too big a concession, but unfortunately failed to spot the other antidote to White's plan. I was also somewhat intrigued by the peculiar idea of ...♘c5 and ...♘d4. But after 13...♘a5!? 14.f4 there is 14...c5!. To be honest, I was sure that any plan involving the move ...♘a5 in order to counter a potential kingside attack was bound to fail, but at this stage, the saying 'beggars can't be choosers' is very appropriate.

14.f4

14.♖b1 f5 15.f4 is very messy, but as in the game, the desperate 15...♗xg1! offers good chances of survival thanks to the ...♕c5, ...♘d4 trick.

14.a5!? was probably the strongest, when after accepting the pawn Black is going to get steamrolled with f4 (though that's also not so simple), while 14...♗c5 15.f4 is the same, but I assume a very slightly better version for White, as I imagine a4-a5 is in most cases a useful extra move.

14...♗xg1! The point of my previous move.

15.♖xg1! White gives up the f4-pawn temporarily, but doesn't allow any ...♕c5, ...♘d4 tricks. After 15.♔xg1, 15...♕c5+! 16.♔h1 ♘d4! solves all problems for Black.

15...exf4 16.d4

Here, 16.♖f1!? concerned me very much as well, because I wasn't sure how good 16...g5 was. But since it looks pretty necessary, I would probably have no choice but to just roll with it.

16...♘e7

I wasn't happy, but at least I had some hopes, now that I transfer my knight to g6 and perhaps will be able to strike with ...c5 at some point.

17.♗a3 ♕d8

The machines don't approve of this move, but facing a central pawn mass as well as the bishop pair, I instinctively wanted to hide my queen so as not to get hit by White's pieces.

17...♕g6 apparently works for Black, introducing the idea of ...♘d5, when after 18.♗d3 (18.♖af1 ♘d5) 18...♕h5, the computer claims that Black is OK. Indeed, it seems the queen manoeuvres have sort of worked out for Black.

18.♖af1 ♘g6

19.e5?

A serious mistake, since now the chances are very high that Black will establish control of the weakened light squares in the centre. I was anticipating 19. g3 with horror, although I must say that I felt rather liberated at this point in the game and was sure I wasn't going to feel any of the pain that was going to be inflicted.

After the game I assumed that 19.g3! would be crushing, but upon closer examination it seems that Black has some very unexpected resources. The way in which the computer puts up a defence is truly impressive: 19...♗h3. This was also the move I was intending (19...fxg3 20.♖xg3 ♕h4 doesn't lose on the spot, but White has a very attractive position), but I am afraid that I didn't even see half the resources that I'd have to find:

20.♖f2. The exchange sac looked very tempting, but this move also poses a very serious question. What's next for Black? (To be honest, I wasn't sure 20.gxf4 was going to come, especially given my opponent's unmatched feel for aesthetics in chess. Still, 20...♗xf1 21.♖xf1 looked very scary, but after 21...♕h4 it's apparently not going to be so easy for White to crash through, since once he starts pushing his pawns forward, Black's knight will get some squares and the computer manages to find adequate counterplay.)

20...♗e6!

ANALYSIS DIAGRAM

A very strong resource, since 21.gxf4 will now be met by the double attack 21...♕h4!.

21.♗d3. Renewing the threat of gxf4, but now the machine-magic continues: 21...f3!, leaving the g1-rook dumbfounded. 22.♖xf3 ♖c8! (22...b6 23.♗b5 is going to be a full exchange after all) and remarkably enough

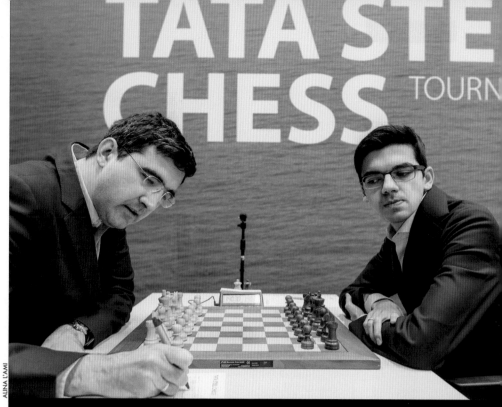

He had no idea about his opponent's plan to retire, but Anish Giri did know that Vladimir Kramnik would aim for adventurous play and possibly grow too optimistic in his desire to be creative.

...c5 is actually coming and Black does get some play for it as well, e.g. 23.♖f2 (moving out of potential ...♘e5's) 23...c5 24.♗xc5, and here the exchange sac is already not so bad, securing very good practical chances to hold the game, thanks to a far superior pawn structure and excellent light pieces. But the first choice of the engine is even more remarkable and perhaps stronger: 24...♕c7!, intending ...♘e5 and ...b6, ♗b4, ...a5, winning the c3-pawn, is on the menu. A sample line: 25.♖c1 ♘e5 26.♗b5 ♖ed8 27.♕b1 b6 28.♗a3 ♘c4, and Black has full positional compensation for the pawn.

19...b6!?
Starting with 19...♗e6 looks more logical, but I wanted to keep the option of going ...♗b7 in some variations after ♗d3.

20.♗f3
I was surprised by this move, as I didn't see any other ideas for White other than going ♗d3 (or ♗e4) and taking on g6, leading to an equal position. Vladimir, however, decided to play for g3!? after all – an ambi-

tious, perhaps overambitious plan, but that was no news.

20...♗a6! 20...♖b8 21.g3!? is probably still more than fine for Black, but it's a much worse version than what I managed to get in the game.

21.♖f2 c5!?
There was no need for this, but I was looking forward to taking over the initiative and didn't bother too much about which move was stronger, as after the exchange sac I didn't think I was taking any risk anyway.

21...♖c8 was perfectly fine as well, when 22.g3 will be met by 22...c5 anyway, and otherwise I can sacrifice an exchange in some other way.

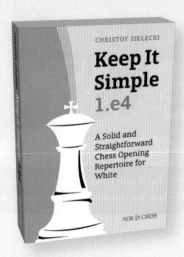

22.g3? I understand White wasn't too thrilled about picking up the exchange, but after going over the options, there is really no other choice but to go for the material. The move in the game is insane, but actually White almost gets rewarded: due to one careless move, I wasted a large part of my advantage.

After 22.♗xa8 ♕xa8 23.♗c1 the computer suggests the sophisticated 23...♕c8!, but after the simple 23...cxd4 24.cxd4 ♖c8 25.♕d1 ♗c4 26.♗xf4 ♗d5 27.♗d2 ♖c4, I would take Black any day of the week, even though I do understand that the light-square domination is most likely only going to be enough for equality, not more. At the end of the day, I don't even have a pawn for the exchange yet.

22...fxg3?! I correctly judged how bad the move 22.g3 actually was, and not seeing any point at all behind it, I actually almost walked into the one and only trap there was.

22...cxd4 23.gxf4 looked a bit vague to me, but after 23...♖c8 24.e6 ♗c4 (24...♖xe6 25.f5 ♖xc3 26.fxe6 ♖xc2 27.exf7+ ♔h8! 28.♖xc2 ♕f6! 29.♗e4 ♕xf7! 30.♖xg6 ♕f4! is a very difficult variation, but Black is completely winning) 25.f5 ♘h4 26.♗e4 ♕f6, Black has the kingside under control and is objectively winning.
23.♖xg3 cxd4 24.cxd4

I already realized that the intended 24....♕xd4 would fail to 25.e6!, so I had to switch to plan B.
24...♖c8!
Regaining my senses. White gets his open files and can protect his d4-pawn, but at the end of the day Black is still a pawn up and has good chances to take over the light squares. 24...♕xd4 25.e6 is really bad news, but for fun I continued calculating the line, just to imagine what would have happened if I had blundered: 25...♖xe6 26.♗xa8 ♖e1+ 27.♖g1 ♖xg1+ 28.♔xg1 ♘f4 29.♔h1 ♘h3 30.♖g2 ♕f6 31.♕d1 ♘f2+ 32.♖xf2 ♕xf2, and Black even has some survival chances.
25.♕f5?
I understand that the temptation to checkmate me in two moves was considerable, but having just almost missed the e6! shot, I wasn't in for a simul-style finale here.
25.♕d2 was simpler and better. White is back in the game, but he doesn't have any scary attack and is objectively probably just slightly worse after 25...♖e6, stabilizing the 6th rank and intending to sac an exchange on d6 if need be. Besides the natural ideas of getting the bishop back to the long diagonal via c4-d5 or simply to b7, Black also has an interesting rook lift idea ...♖c7-♖d7, which I quite like.

story in the making? Two youngsters who want to become World Champion, Praggnanandhaa and Parham Maghsoodloo, have a go at Magnus Carlsen and Ian Nepomniachtchi.

the queen and the g7-rook are in the wrong positions. White will be unable to deliver the needed blow and 31.♖fg2 is met by 31...♕f4!, when Black is in control and has a winning advantage.

30...♘f4 31.♖d4

31.♗f8 ♖xf8 32.♖xd8 ♖fxd8 is dead lost for White, since 33.♖xg7 is met by 33...♘h3, followed (if the queen leaves the first rank) by 34...♖c1+ and 35...♖g1 mate.

31...♘g6

After picking up the d-pawn the knight simply returns and the rest is just about getting to the time-control.

32.♗e4 ♖c4

Trading off pieces makes things easier.

33.♖xc4 ♗xc4 34.♕d4 ♗e6
35.♗c6 ♘e7 Simplifying further.
36.♗e4 36.♗xe8 is met by 36...♘f5!.
36...♘f5 37.♗xf5 ♗xf5 38.♔g1
♗e6 39.h4 ♕d7 40.♕e4 ♗c8
41.h5 ♖c1+ 42.♔h2 ♕d8

25...♗c4! A mood spoiler. Now Black is in firm control once again and the rest is a matter of staying tactically alert and keeping a cool head.
25...♕xd4?? 26.♕xf7+ ♔xf7 27.♗d5 mate, is very pretty indeed!
26.♗d6 ♗e6 27.♕b1

27...♘f4 I had originally planned 27...♖c3, which turns out to be good

as well, but this is cleaner, aiming for the crucial d5-square and not fearing any ghosts along the g-file.

28.d5 ♘xd5 29.♕g1

This move works better against ...g5, as after 29.h4 Black no longer gets the ♘f4/♘e3 tempo, but now there is another antidote.

After 29.♖fg2 g5! 30.h4 both 30...♘f4 and 30...♘e3 win, since once a black rook gets to the h-file, it's no longer clear who is actually attacking.

29...♔h8!

Black could also start with 29...♕h4.

30.♖d2

Taking on g7 wouldn't lead anywhere, but this doesn't work either.

After 30.♖xg7 the prosaic 30...♖g8 is good enough, but I was actually planning to go for 30...♕h4, when

And having all good pieces exchanged and with a two-pawn deficit and now also a mating attack coming, White had no choice but to resign.

■ ■ ■

With this win, Giri had caught up with Carlsen again, and two rounds later, after beating Richard Rapport in Round 4, again with the black pieces, he even drew half a point ahead, because Carlsen had made his fourth draw, extending his drawing streak – which obviously also included the 12 draws in London against Caruana – to an unprecedented 21. Giri didn't miss this opportunity to congratulate him on his new record on Twitter.

Carlsen not only needed a win to start playing for tournament victory, he was also leaking Elo points. In the live ratings, the gap between him and Caruana had dwindled to just 3 points. No doubt to the Champion's relief, it didn't get smaller, because in the next round, Jorden van Foreest lent a helping hand by challenging him in the Sveshnikov, which Carlsen had studied in great depth for the world title match. There was actually nothing wrong with the Dutchman's position after the opening, but when he declined to take a pawn for which Black would have got only dubious compensation, he was soon blown away by an invasion of the black pieces.

In the rounds that followed, Carlsen won two more games, against Rapport and against Shakhriyar Mamedyarov (in an endgame that you will find, together with other endgame feats of the World Champion, in Jan Timman's column on page 102), and after Round 9 the Norwegian was topping the table together with Ian Nepomniachtchi and Vishy Anand, half a point ahead of Ding Liren and Giri.

Let's walk

Carlsen has always felt at home in Wijk aan Zee, and this time was no different. Together with his parents he was staying in a spacious apartment close to the sea. One day, he even went for a swim in the North Sea, together with his second Peter Heine Nielsen. As has become his wont, he very much stuck to himself

and only left his private circle for the rounds and for a basketball game on the second free day. He clearly demonstrated how much he prefers to be left alone when he got upset about a photographer who kept annoying him during the basketball game. At some point, he had had enough and left, leaving Nielsen guessing where he had gone. As it turned out, he had been so angry that he had not looked for anyone or waited for his car, but had walked straight back to Wijk aan Zee (nine kilometres!).

The next day, he punished all other photographers – the culprit had already been banned by the organ-

'Carlsen had been so angry that he had not looked for his car but walked straight back to Wijk aan Zee (9 kilometres!).'

izers – by appearing 10 minutes late. His opponent, Mamedyarov, seemed unaffected and also waited 10 minutes before he made his first move.

Mamedyarov was unrecognizable in Wijk aan Zee. Seeded second, the Azeri GM didn't win a single game and lost three, losing his 2800+ rating in the process by dropping a whopping 23 points. Perhaps that explains why he could often be seen in one of the bars, trying to forget about his games by playing blitz (giving extreme time odds) against all comers deep into the night.

How different was his compatriot's performance. Teimour Radjabov was having a good time and showed flashes of his old self again. If there had been a beauty prize, his win against Vidit Gujrathi would have been a serious candidate.

NOTES BY
Teimour Radjabov

Teimour Radjabov
Vidit Gujrathi
Wijk aan Zee 2019 (7)
Queen's Gambit Declined,
Ragozin Variation

Vidit has a solid repertoire as Black – like more or less everyone else at top level – but I only discovered after this game that g2-g4 as early as possible and almost in any position yields me winning chances ☺.
1.d4 ♘f6 2.c4 e6 3.♘f3 d5 4.♘c3 ♗b4 5.♕a4+ ♘c6 6.e3 0-0 7.♕c2 ♖e8

Black is trying to push ...e5, and his preparation starts with this move.
8.♗d2 ♗d6?!
Vidit is mixing up the move order. A better way for Black is to start with 8...a6!, as now I could have played c5!.

9.h3?!
I was also sure that we were doing it right and played h3 fast. As Vidit has a good relationship with Giri, I just wonder whether Vidit is a hypnotizer as well? ☺
After 9.c5! ♗f8 10.♗b5, Black is

already worse and White's play is much easier.

9...a6 10.a3

Strange moves, in order to capture on c4 at once with the bishop, without wasting time on ♗e2 or ♗d3.

10...♗d7 After this White has to develop the f1-bishop.

11.♗e2 dxc4 12.♗xc4 h6

As in my notes to this variation, I was going g4 everywhere. I just thought, 'What is going on if I go g4 here as well? ...h6 has been played, it's time to attack!'

13.g4!?

13...e5?

I think this is a very unpractical decision. Clearly, White is going to attack with g5, and the bishop is very strong now on the a2-g8 diagonal. I was happy about 13...e5 and thought I was winning by force. The computer suggests 13...b5!, which seems to solve all Black's problems at once!

After 13...b5! 14.♗d3, Black has a choice:

ANALYSIS DIAGRAM

A) Here 14...e5?! is far more natural, but I am not a fan of Black's position after 15.d5. White is ready to sacrifice

Teimour Radjabov played a lovely attacking game worthy of a beauty prize.

this pawn for the attack, of course! 15...♗e7 16.g5 hxg5 17.♘xg5 ♘exd5 18.♘xd5 ♘xd5 19.h4! ♘f6 20.0-0-0, and it's important that the pawn is on h4: h5 is coming; this is practically lost for Black.

B) But better is 14...♕e7!, when ...e5-e4 is a threat, but it's a move that is hard to spot when g5 seems to be the threat: 15.g5 (15.♘e4 e5!, and ...♘d4 is always in the air) 15...hxg5 16.♘xg5 e5 17.d5

ANALYSIS DIAGRAM

and now:

B1) If 17...♘d4 then 18.exd4 exd4+ 19.♘e2 ♗f5! 20.♕b3!; otherwise ...♕xe2 – 20...a5!!. This would be hard to see, but it's beautiful. Now White's

best move is 21.♗c1! (in order to meet 21...a4 with 22.♕d1!) 21...♘xd5! 22.♔f1. This looks like ending up in equality, but come on! ☺

B2) 17...e4!?, and let's look at two options here:

B21) 18.♗xe4 ♘xe4 19.♘cxe4 ♗f5!?. The most natural way for Black. 20.♕xc6 ♗xe4 21.♘xe4 ♕xe4 22.0-0-0 a5, with great compensation for Black and a dynamically balanced position.

B22) 18.♘cxe4 ♘e5 19.♘xd6 ♘xd3+ 20.♕xd3 ♕xd6 looks like the more human way to neutralize the attack: 21.♖c1, with equality.

14.g5

14...b5

We were very critical of this move in our post-mortem, but actually it's the best one! 14...exd4?! is OK for Black, but it's impossible to find the sequence of moves to keep the balance: 15.gxh6 ♗e6! 16.♗xe6 ♖xe6 17.♖g1 ♗h5 18.♘e2 ♖xh6 19.♘exd4 ♘xd4 20.♘xd4

ANALYSIS DIAGRAM

20...♗h2! There is no chess player I know capable of playing like this, but anyway, it's the best move! 21.♖g4 ♘f6 22.♖g2 ♗e5 23.♘f5 ♖g6 24.♖xg6 fxg6 25.♘h4 g5 26.♘f5 ♕e8!!, and by going ...♘e4 next, compy claims that Black is fine.

15.♗a2

15...exd4?

Very interesting was 15...♘xd4!?, with great lines to follow. This was objectively keeping the equality for Black: 16.exd4 exd4+ 17.♘e2 ♕e7 18.♘fxd4 hxg5 19.♗e3 ♗f4!! 20.♗xf4 gxf4 21.♕g6 c5 (the only move!) 22.♖g1 ♘g4 (the only move again! White wins after 22...♗g4 23.hxg4 cxd4 24.0-0-0 ♖ac8+ 25.♔b1) 23.hxg4 cxd4 24.0-0-0 ♖ac8+, and now, after 25.♔b1, 25...♖c6!! is more or less the point of 22...♘g4 ! – the queen on g6

is attacked. 26.♕h5 ♖h6 27.♕d5 ♗e6 28.♕xd4 ♗xa2+ 29.♔xa2 ♕xe2 and this should end in a draw.

16.gxh6 This seemed very strong to me, and I even thought that I would be able to mate Black with ♕g6 sooner or later ☺.

I also thought about 16.0-0-0!?, but only very briefly. I thought it should not work, as White is sacrificing too much too fast. Actually, it was very interesting. To begin with, I had not seen Black's reply 16...b4!! 17.gxh6 ♗e6!

ANALYSIS DIAGRAM

18.♘d5!!. An amazing move meant to distract Black's pieces from the kingside. After this very annoying trick Black has to be a genius to keep the balance: 18...♘xd5 19.♖dg1 ♕f6 20.♖xg7+ ♔f8 21.♘g5 ♕xh6 22.♖xf7+!! ♗xf7 23.♘xf7 ♕f6!! (what a defence!!) 24.♗xd5 ♘e7! 25.♗c4!? bxa3 26.exd4 ♗f4 27.♖g1! ♗xd2+ 28.♕xd2 ♘c6, and there are plenty of tries here for White, but all of them lead to a draw... believe me.
16...dxc3? 16...♗f4!! was a really great defensive idea here. Black is attacking h6 and e3 and White should

forget about a direct attack and switch to more positional play. This idea was suggested to us during our post-mortem. I had seen it during the game, but thought that White should still have something here: 17.0-0-0! ♗xh6 18.exd4 ♗xd2+ 19.♕xd2 b4!, and now all attempts to destroy Black's kingside will fail, for instance 20.axb4 ♘xb4 21.♗c4 ♗c6 (the only move) 22.♘g5 ♗d5 23.♘xd5 ♘bxd5 24.h4 ♖b8 25.h5 ♘e4, with equality.

17.♗xc3 I was very upset that 17.♕g6 does not work as I had concluded while Vidit was thinking. But I had this move in reserve, with a very strong attack! After 17.♕g6? cxd2+ 18.♔e2 ♗f8 19.♗xf7+ ♔h8 20.hxg7+ ♗xg7 21.♖hg1 ♖g8 22.♖g4 ♗xg4 23.hxg4 ♘h7!, Black is winning in all lines thanks to ...d1♕ check after White goes ♖h1.
17...♗e6? This seems pretty natural, but in fact it is losing due to a great move by White.
17...♗f4 was still the best move, but here White is close to winning after 18.♖d1! ♗xh6 19.♕g6 ♕e7 20.♗xf6 ♕xf6 21.♕xf6 gxf6 22.♖xd7.

18.♗xe6?

I had thought about 18.♖g1!!, but my rook seemed placed too badly on a2. That's why I decided to play 18.♗xe6, to keep the 0-0-0 option open. In fact, this great move would have been directly winning! 18...♗xa2. Believe it or not, but even 19.♖xa2 wins here! It's important that Black's rook on e8 is not helping the defence: 19.♖xg7+ ♔f8 20.♖xa2 ♗e5 (this position had seemed unclear to me) 21.♘g5 ♕d5 22.♖xf7+ ♕xf7 23.♘xf7 ♔xf7 24.a4. Now don't ask me why, but this move is very important to claim victory for White: 24...b4 25.♗xe5 ♘xe5 26.♖a1. The rook is back in the game and Black's position is hopeless after ♕b3+, ♔e2, f4, ♖g1, etc.

18...♖xe6 19.♖g1 In my calculations, Black had to go ...♘e8, but in fact he had an amazing resource!

19...♘e8?? The move I had expected, but there was 19...♘h5!! 20.♗xg7 ♗g3!!. All these beautiful resources to still get a much worse position, you will say? Well... practically speaking, this could completely turn the tables. It's very hard to find the best moves for White: 21.♔e2!? ♕e7 22.♗c3 ♖xh6 23.♕f5

and now the idea of White is to go ♘h2-♘f1 ☺.

20.♗xg7 ♘xg7 21.♖xg7+ ♔f8 22.♕h7! ♕f6 23.♘g5

White is completely winning.

23...♖xe3+ The last trick. 23...♘d8 loses to 24.♕g8+ ♔e7 25.h7.

24.♔f1

A blunder would be 24.fxe3?? ♗g3+ 25.♔d1 ♕f1+ 26.♔c2, and Black secures the draw.

24...♘d8

After 24...♘e5!? 25.♕g8+ ♔e7 26.♕xa8 ♗c5 27.♕g2, White protects f2, and Black's position is left in ruins: 27...♕xh6 28.♖g8.

25.♕g8+ ♔e7 26.h7 ♗g3 27.♘e4! ♖xe4 28.♖xg3 ♖h4 29.♖d1

Black is helpless, as ♖e3+ is coming. There are plenty of wins for White, but this seems to be the simplest one.
29...♖xh7 30.♖e3+ ♘e6 31.♕xa8 ♖h8 32.♕c6 ♔f8

33.♖xe6 Always nice to make such a move. **33...♕xe6 34.♖d8+ ♔g7**
Now, after 35.♕xe6, the pawn ending would be utterly winning, but being a rook up is more pleasant!
35.♕c3+ f6 36.♕xc7+

Black resigned. A very satisfying game; sharp, beautiful and attacking, the type of chess I enjoy the most!

∎ ∎ ∎

As said, after nine rounds Vishy Anand was one of the leaders and had reason to hope for a sensation. With five victories, the former World Champion is the most successful participant in Wijk aan Zee after Magnus Carlsen. In Round 7, he won a crazy game against his old friend and rival Kramnik, levelling their lifetime score in classical games to 11-11. Would he be able to fight for first place once more, now that he was winning games like the following, in Round 8, with such ease?

NOTES BY
Vishy Anand

Vishy Anand
Shakhriyar Mamedyarov
Wijk aan Zee 2019 (8)
Caro-Kann Defence, Advance Variation

1.e4 c6 One of his favourite openings, so no surprise there.
2.d4 d5 3.e5 c5
This, however, is new from him; he has only played 3...♗f5 before.
4.dxc5 e6 5.♘f3 ♗xc5 6.a3 ♘e7 7.♗d3 ♘g6 8.0-0 0-0 9.♘bd2 ♘c6 10.b4 ♗b6

11.♗xg6 11.♗b2 ♘f4 transposes to my game as Black against Vitiugov at the 2018 Grenke Classic. I remember being quite comfortable in that game. The other move is 11.♖e1, when Black has a choice:

ANALYSIS DIAGRAM

A) 11...♘cxe5 12.♘xe5 ♘xe5 13.♖xe5 ♗d4, when chances would be equal after 14.♘f3, 14.♖e3 and 14.♖h5.
B) 11...♘f4 12.♘b3 – the point of ♖e1, White's bishop is well placed on c1.
C) 11...f6. This is simpler to play: 12.♗xg6 hxg6 13.♗b2 ♘xe5 14.♗xe5 fxe5 15.♖xe5 ♕f6 16.♕e1.

11...fxg6 After 11...hxg6, 12.♖b1 is a good suggestion by the engine: 12...g5 13.b5 ♘a5 14.♖b4! – a clever way to exploit ...g5.
12.♘b3

12...♗d7
I was relieved to see this.
12...a5 bothered me a bit: 13.b5 a4! (the point) 14.bxc6 axb3 15.c7! (the best way to return the pawn) 15...♕xc7 16.cxb3 ♗d7 17.♖e1, and White should be able to blockade on d4, but isn't really better.
13.♖e1 a5?! 14.b5 ♘e7
14...a4 doesn't work now: 15.bxc6 axb3 16.cxd7.
15.a4

Here I started liking my position, since my pawns on b5 and a4 restrict the ♗d7, enabling me to occupy d4.
15...♖c8 16.♗e3 ♗xe3 17.♖xe3
My optimism notwithstanding, Black is extremely solid here.
17...♘f5 Both 17...g5 18.h3 b6 19.♖d3 h6, when it's hard for White to make progress, and 17...♖f4 18.♕d2 (White won't be in time with 18.♘fd4 ♘f5! 19.♖d3 ♘xd4 20.♘xd4 ♖e4) 18...♖b4! are fine for Black.
18.♖d3

After 9 rounds Vishy Anand was one of the leaders and could secretly dream of a sixth overall victory in Wijk aan Zee.

Chess on Tour

As in the past few years, the Tata Steel tournament went on tour for two rounds. This time, Alkmaar and Leiden had earned the right to stage a round, and both days were a resounding success. Round 10 took place in the Pieterskerk in the heart of Leiden, a city famous for having the oldest university of the Netherlands, founded in 1575. The setting was perfect for what turned out to be a key round. The main victims were two of the leaders, Anand and Nepomniachtchi. In the longest game of the day, Anand was ground down by Magnus Carlsen – a game that the Indian understandably called 'a disaster'. The endgame he lost you will also find in Jan Timman's column. Carlsen's will to win was admirable and so was his play, but it is tempting to say that his opponent

'The setting in the Pieterskerk in the centre of Leiden was perfect for what turned out to be a key round.'

would have defended better if the game had been played earlier in the tournament.

The other leader, Nepomniachtchi, tried to confuse Van Foreest by giving away a tempo in a sharp opening – a daring ploy, except that it backfired badly. Jorden van Foreest, rated 2612, faced an arduous task in his top group debut, but he was spoiling for a fight each time and played several games he could be proud of. His win against 'Nepo' was one of three wins he will cherish for some time.

18...g5? A natural move, but an error. Correct was 18...♘h4! 19.♘xh4 ♕xh4 20.♕d2 b6. **19.h3** Threatening a fork with ♕d2. **19...b6** 19...♕c7 20.c4 ♕xc4 21.♘xa5 is a good pawn swap for White.

20.c4! The point. **20...♖xc4 21.♖xd5 ♖f7 22.♖d3 g4 23.♘fd2** Now it's over. **23...♗b4 24.hxg4 ♘e7 25.♗f3** 25.♘c4 ♘g6 26.♘bd2 was even stronger.

25...♘d5 26.♘bd4 Now Shakh blunders immediately, but the game was won anyway.

26...♖f4? 27.♘c2! ♖be4 Or 27...♖xa4 28.♖xa4 ♖xa4 29.♖xd5 exd5 30.♕xd5+ ♔f8 31.e6, and White wins. **28.♖xd5 exd5 29.♕xd5+**

And Black resigned, since White will follow up with ♖d1, collecting the ♗d7.

NOTES BY
Jorden van Foreest

**Jorden van Foreest
Ian Nepomniachtchi**
Wijk aan Zee 2019 (10)
Sicilian Defence, Najdorf Variation

Playing in the Masters of the Tata Steel Chess Tournament was a fantastic experience. This game, played in the 'On Tour' round in Leiden, was the highlight of my tournament, and I am happy to show it to you.
1.e4 c5 2.♘f3 d6 3.d4 cxd4 4.♘xd4 ♘f6 5.♘c3 a6 The Najdorf is Nepomniachtchi's main weapon and he rarely deviates from it.
6.h3 This might have come as a surprise to my opponent, since I have been playing 6.♗e2 recently.
6...e5 7.♘b3 ♗e6 8.f4

8...exf4?!
I don't understand why my opponent chose to play this move. By taking on f4 he gives me an extra tempo in a well-known main line, which even with an extra move isn't easy for Black. Needless to say, I was pleasantly surprised.
8...♗e7 9.♗e3 exf4 10.♗xf4 is how the line usually goes, when White has moved his bishop twice, so Black has gained a tempo compared to the game.
9.♗xf4 ♘c6 10.♕e2 ♗e7 11.0-0-0 ♕c7 12.g4 0-0 13.g5 ♘d7 14.♕e3
This move wasn't entirely necessary. Better was to start pushing pawns with 14.h4 directly, when the engines already give White a huge advantage of around +2.

14...♖ac8 15.♔b1 ♖fe8
The development of the rook is quite natural, but in this case it doesn't quite meet the demands of the position. Black had to act more quickly, trying to achieve counterplay by means of putting a knight on c4. 15...♘ce5 16.h4 ♘b6 would have been similar to the game, but a better version for Black. The idea of ...♘bc4 creates threats that give Black some counterplay.
16.h4 b5

17.♕g3 Not a bad move, getting out of the e-file and away from possible jumps from a black knight to c4.
The computer, however, points out that it was possible to go for the kill immediately: 17.♗h3! ♘b6 (after 17...b4 18.♘d5 ♗xd5 19.exd5 ♗xg5

'He gives me an extra tempo in a well-known main line, which even with an extra move isn't easy for Black.'

20.♕f2 ♗xf4 21.dxc6 ♗e3 22.♕f3, White is winning) 18.g6! hxg6 19.♗xe6 fxe6 20.♕h3, and with e6 hanging and h5 coming, White's attack is crushing.
17...♘ce5 18.♘d4 ♘b6 19.♗h3 ♗xh3 20.♕xh3 ♘ec4

Black has finally managed to create a threat: 21...♘xb2, but this is easily dealt with.
21.♘d5 ♘xd5 22.exd5 ♘b6
This move was played quickly, and I must confess I had missed it. It turns out that it is impossible to defend the pawn on d5 correctly. After thinking for a while I decided to give up the pawn in order to retain a strong attack.

23.♗c1
23.♕g2 ♕c4 24.♘f5, with the point of sacrificing the knight on h6, was an idea which caught my interest for a moment, but I soon realized it wouldn't work: 24...♕xf4 25.♖hf1 (25.♘h6+ gxh6 26.gxh6+ ♗g5, and Black wins) 25...♕e5 26.♖de1 ♕xd5, and Black can always interpose his bishop on g5 in case of ♘h6+: 27.♘h6+ gxh6 28.gxh6+ ♗g5, and Black remains a piece up.

After 23.♘c6?, 23...♘xd5! is Black's main point.

23...♘xd5

24.h5

24.♕f3! would have been a more precise continuation, attacking the black knight, while at the same time hitting the weak f7 point in Black's camp: 24...♘b4 (24...♘b6 25.h5, and with the knight gone from the centre, the attack only becomes stronger) 25.♖hf1 ♗f8 26.c3 ♘c6 27.♘xc6 ♕xc6 28.♕xf7+, winning.

24...♗f8 25.g6 h6 26.♕g2

Immediately after the game I thought this had been a mistake, giving my opponent an opportunity to get back into the game. After returning home and some analysis, I realized that the move is not that bad after all.

26...♘f6?

This is a blunder that allows me to blast the black kingside open.
Black's best chance was 26...♘e3!. During the game I thought that this was impossible due to a quick ♘f5, but it turns out Black can survive: 27.♗xe3 ♖xe3 28.♖hf1!. The correct approach, aiming for a positional bind

As chief arbiter Pavel Votruba registers the Dutchman's win by putting the kings on the right central squares, Jorden van Foreest suggests an improvement to Ian Nepomniachtchi.

(after 28.♘f5 ♖e6! covers the sixth rank and saves the day for Black). Even the engines need some time to realize that Black is still in serious trouble: 28...f6 29.♖fe1 ♖e5 30.♖xe5 dxe5 31.♘f5, and although Black is a pawn up, White's positional compensation is so good that he is still far better.

27.♗xh6!

27...fxg6

27...gxh6? 28.gxf7+ ♔xf7 29.♕g6+ ♔e7 30.♖he1+ is not a possibility.
27...♖e4 was a move suggested by my opponent directly after the game, but it doesn't help Black either: 28.♗xg7! ♗xg7 29.h6 ♖g4 30.♕f2 fxg6 31.hxg7

♕xg7 32.♕h2, with a devastating attack.

28.♖df1?! Deploying another piece looks logical, but there was a cleaner way to victory: 28.♗g5! ♘xh5 29.♗c1!. After forcing Black to take the pawn on h5, the bishop retreats with deadly effect. The pawn on g6 will soon fall, bringing down the black position.

28...♕c4 I thought that 28...♕e7, with the idea of ...♕e4, was a good defensive try, but there is a beautiful refutation: 29.♖xf6! ♕xf6 30.♗g5! ♕xd4 31.hxg6, and there is absolutely nothing Black can do to prevent mate on the h-file.

29.♖xf6 ♕xd4 30.♖xg6

30...♔h7? A last mistake, after which White is able to break through. After the more resilient 30...♖c7, I didn't see a clear way to break through yet – and as it turns out, there wasn't any.

31.♗c1 ♕e4

Swapping the queens would be great for Black, but he is just too late...

32.h6! This strong move throws a

spanner in Black's works. All files towards the black king are being opened, and there is no escape.

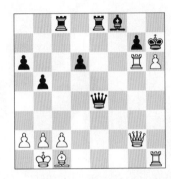

32...♕xg6 After 32...♕xg2 33.hxg7+ ♔xg6 34.g8♕+ ♗g7, 35.♖h6+! is the key move which had to be calculated, after which Black swiftly gets mated: 35...♔f5 36.♕f7+ ♔e4 37.♕f4+ ♔d5 38.♖xd6+ ♔c5 39.b4 mate.

33.hxg7+ ♔xg7 34.♗h6+ ♔f7 35.♖f1+ ♕f6 36.♕d5+

36...♔e7
To survive a little longer Black has to sacrifice his queen, but the resulting position will be hopeless.

A nice way to end the game would have been 36...♔g6 37.♖g1+ ♔xh6 38.♕h1+ ♕h4 39.♕xh4 mate.

37.♗g5 ♕xg5 38.♖f7+ ♔d8 39.♕xg5+ ♗e7 40.♕d5

Having won the queen and with the black king still in danger, the win is just a matter of time and technique. Although my converting skills were far from perfect, I managed to get there in the end.

40...♖g8 41.a3 ♖g1+ 42.♔a2 ♖e1 43.♕b7
It wasn't necessary to give up the c2-pawn. 43.c3 would have been slightly easier.

43...♖xc2 44.♖h7 ♖c7 45.♕xa6 ♖e5 46.♖h8+ ♔d7 47.♕a8

♗f6 48.♖f8 ♗g7 49.♖d8+ ♔e7
50.♕b8 ♖ec5 51.♖g8 ♔e6
52.♕e8+ ♔d5 53.♕e2 ♗e5

After going in circles for some time, I realized that the easiest way to win this position would be to capture the b5-pawn and queen one of my remaining pawns.

**54.♖b8 ♔c6 55.♕e4+ ♔d7
56.♕d3 ♔c6 57.♕f3+**

57...d5

By trying to keep his pawn, Black has to expose his king even more. 57...♔d7 58.♕f7+ ♔c6 59.♕e8+ ♔d5 60.♖xb5 is an easy for win for White.

**58.♕h5 d4 59.♕g6+ ♗d6
60.♕e4+**

Black is bound to lose material, so my opponent resigned.

■ ■ ■

Nepomniachtchi wasn't the only Russian to lose in Round 10. As it happened, all three of them lost. Vidit Gujrathi, the winner of last year's Challengers, was in an aggressive mood against Kramnik, and saw his attacking play pay off.

NOTES BY
Vidit Gujrathi

**Vidit Gujrathi
Vladimir Kramnik**
Wijk aan Zee 2019 (10)
Nimzo-Indian Defence, Sämisch Variation

Two days after the Tata Steel Chess Tournament, Vladimir Kramnik announced his decision to retire from chess. Although he was far from his best form in Wijk aan Zee, I am lucky that I got a chance to play against the legend himself. In fact, he was the only player from the participants whom I hadn't faced before.

1.d4 ♘f6 2.c4 e6 3.♘c3 ♗b4 4.f3

This game was played in Round 10. After a successful first half I had scored only half a point in the next three games (yes, ironically that half point was against Anish Giri!). So I very much wanted to get back into the event, and with this move I was aiming for an open fight with all three possible results in mind.

**4...d5 5.a3 ♗xc3+ 6.bxc3 c5
7.cxd5 exd5**

I was a bit surprised by this choice. Although this line was used by Magnus Carlsen to defeat Vishy Anand in their first World Championship match, it never really caught on.

8.e3 c4 9.♘e2 ♘c6 10.g4

10...♘a5 Carlsen went for castling first and then the same plan with ...♘a5-b3: 10...0-0 11.♗g2 ♘a5 12.0-0 ♘b3 13.♖a2 b5 14.♘g3 a5 15.g5 ♘e8 16.e4 ♘xc1 17.♕xc1 ♖a6 18.e5 ♘c7 19.f4 b4 20.axb4 axb4 21.♖xa6 ♘xa6 22.f5 b3 23.♕f4 ♘c7 24.f6 g6 25.♕h4 ♘e8 26.♕h6 b2 27.♖f4 b1♕+ 28.♘f1?? ♕e1, 0-1; Anand-Carlsen, Chennai 2013.

11.♗g2 ♘b3 12.♖b1

A novelty for over-the-board games. As this game was played on one of the Chess on Tour days, we had to leave earlier than usual. While walking towards the bus, my coach informed me that the rook on b1 is better placed for a quick e2-e4. That's all I knew about this line.

12...0-0 13.0-0 b5?!

This opens the h1-a8 diagonal. Starting with the counter-intuitive 13...a5 seems better. One advantage is that Black can play ...♖a6 and bring the rook in the game.

Vidit Gujrathi aimed for an open fight 'with all three possible results in mind'.
No doubt Vladimir Kramnik had similar plans, but this was the Indian's game.

14.e4!
I played this pawn sacrifice after thinking for five minutes. For one pawn White gets a lot of initiative, so it was not hard for me to convince myself. Peter Leko also remarked in the live commentary that it doesn't even feel as if White is a pawn down!
14...dxe4 15.fxe4

15...♘xc1 Played instantly. I was a little surprised by the speed of his play. If it was his preparation, I didn't understand what I was missing.
15...♗xg4 felt more natural, but the resulting position looks ugly: 16.♗g5 ♕b6 17.♗xf6 gxf6 18.♕e1 (getting out of the pin) 18...♗xe2 19.♕xe2 ♔h8 20.♔h1, and now I just double rooks on the f-file and sooner or later play e5. What can Black do?
16.♕xc1 ♗xg4 17.♘f4 ♖b8 18.h3! An important point. The immediate 18.e5 would allow 18...♘h5, when White loses some momentum.

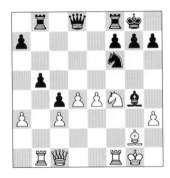

18...♗d7 After the game Kramnik told me that he had mixed up his preparation and that he had 18...♗c8 in his notes. Either I don't understand

the position or he mixed up some different line. White's play is still very easy after 18...♗c8 19.e5 ♘d7 20.♕e3. 18...♗e6 makes more sense. Immediately pushing the pawns leaves the centre fragile. White has to make some preparatory moves like ♕e3/♖be1 and then play d5/e5: 19.♕e3! (after 19.d5?! ♗c8 20.e5 ♘d7 21.♕e3 ♕b6 is the point) 19...a5 20.♔h2, followed by d5/e5, with a clear advantage for White.

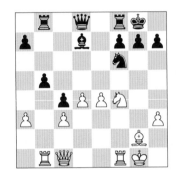

19.e5! I played this intuitively. Apparently move order is important. If I had played ♕e3 first, Black would have had extra defensive possibilities: 19.♕e3 ♔h8! 20.e5 ♘g8. Too cheeky for me to see.
19...♘e8 20.♕e3

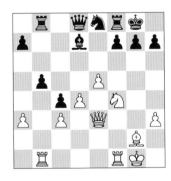

Finally, after this move Kramnik had a long think. I feel the position is already very difficult for Black. I once read an interesting comment about Fischer's play: 'His plans are simple and straightforward but at the same time very hard to stop.' The current position gives a very similar vibe. I am just going to push my central pawns, and I don't see how Black can prevent it.

20...♖b6 21.d5 ♘c7 22.d6

I was aware of the classic Kasparov-Pribyl, European Team Championship 1980,

Kasparov-Pribyl
Skara 1980
position after 19...f6

in which Kasparov played 20.d7!, cutting the board in half. There followed: 20...fxg5 21.♕c4+ ♚h8 22.♘xg5 ♗f6 23.♘e6 ♘c7 24.♘xf8 ♖xf8 25.♖d6 ♗e7 26.d8♕ ♗xd8 27.♕c3+ ♚g8 28.♖d7 ♗f6 29.♕c4+ ♚h8 30.♕f4 ♕a6 31.♕h6 1-0.
So, the decision to allow ...♘e6 at the cost of dividing Black's defences was an easy one to make.

22...♘e6 23.♘d5 ♖a6

24.♖f5!

It was important to stop ...♕g5. Now I have threats like ♖h5, ♘e7+ and ♗e4. The attack just plays itself.

24...♕h4 25.♖bf1

White is winning.

25...♖xa3 26.♘e7+ ♚h8 27.♖xf7 ♖xf7 28.♖xf7

I have threats like ♕f3 and ♖f8. Black is not in time to create any counterplay with the rook.

28...♕h5 29.♕f4!

A cute finish! Black resigned. After the game, my coach Alon Greenfeld and I were walking down the vibrant streets of Leiden, when suddenly a stranger walked up to us and asked if I was Vidit. Upon confirmation, he congratulated me on the game and the final move. That's what makes Tata Steel Chess such a special event! ☺

And what about Anish Giri? Did he still have a chance to compete with Magnus Carlsen in the fight for first place? He certainly kept these hopes alive when he remained cool-headed in a complicated tussle with Vladimir Fedoseev.

NOTES BY
Anish Giri

**Vladimir Fedoseev
Anish Giri**
Wijk aan Zee 2019 (10)
Sicilian Defence, Closed Variation

1.e4 c5 2.♘c3 Nowadays it is no longer shocking when White tries his luck in a sub-line in hopes of surprising his opponent. And why not?

2...d6 3.♘ge2 ♘f6 4.g3
It was still not too late to come back to one's senses and go 4.d4.

4...g6 5.♗g2 ♘c6 6.d3
Here 6.d4 is already less attractive, as Black gets the chance to play the Dragon without committing to ...a6, having avoided the dangerous set-up with ♗e3, f3 and ♕d2.

6...♗g7 7.h3 0-0 8.♗e3?!

I was more familiar with set-ups that do not involve the development of this bishop, having watched my wife's video series on the topic of the Closed Sicilian. I believe she doesn't recommend this move here.

8...♖b8 9.f4 ♘e8?!

I was thinking about whether to play this or ...♘d7. I finally went for the text, because I thought it would give me easier play.

Indeed, after 9...♘d7 the knight is already on its ideal square, ready for the eventual ...f5 push, when it will control the key squares f6 and e5. On e8, however, the knight stands very poorly, but I can spend three more moves rerouting it to d4 via c7 and b5 (or e6). These are three easy moves I couldn't resist.

10.a4 ♘d4
Too clever. 10...♘c7 followed by ...b5 would give me easier play.

11.0-0

Once I had placed the knight on d4, I kept expecting a move like ♗f2 or ♗d2, creating the positional threat of ♘xd4, after which I would trade on e2. This, however, never happened, so I never really got to trade on e2.

11...♘c7 12.g4 a6

I felt my last few moves, and especially the order in which they were made, weren't entirely consistent, but as they were all serving some sort of purpose they shouldn't be too bad either.

13.♖b1

This move, just like most of the moves in this game, was not something I had expected, but it does make quite some sense. First of all, White is now always ready to meet ...♘xe2 with ♘xe2 if he wishes to do so, and, secondly, the idea of meeting ...b5 with axb5 ...axb5 b4 gets introduced.

13...♗d7

I felt this was once again too clever, but it shouldn't be bad either.

Here, after 13...b5 14.axb5 axb5 (I dismissed 14...♘cxb5 on account of the simple 15.♘xb5, when I felt White is going to be just an inch

better: 15.♘xb5 ♘xe2+ 16.♕xe2, and now it is possible to take 'positionally' with the pawn. But Black can also take with the rook and then try to get rid of the weak a6-pawn with ...a5-a4) 15.b4 is a decent idea for White, intending to fight for some central squares via the queenside.

14.♘g3

Not sure this was best, as now I could have replied with 14...e6!?, preventing White's main idea of pushing f4-f5.

14...b5

I made this and the subsequent two moves very quickly and superficially. Only after I had made them did I realize that the position that I was aiming for is not at all clear.

Better was 14...e6!? 15.♕d2 (15.f5? is now simply met by 15...♗e5!, when White's play backfires, since he is not going to be able to support his pawn avalanche with proper piece play), and now Black can go 15...f5!? 16.gxf5 exf5, and it feels as though Black has managed to take the sting out of White's play.

15.axb5 axb5 16.♘ce2 b4 17.f5

My first impression here was that now that I had got ...b5-b4 and I am ready to follow up with ...♘cb5, all my previous moves sort of made sense and it was time for my play to actually lead somewhere. The more I thought

about the position, however, the more I realized that I had once again treated the position in the style of Fritz 5.32 instead of playing in the style of the crowd's favourite, AlphaZero. The ...b4-b3 push is always met by c3 and won't yield me anything, while White has much easier play on the kingside. I wasn't entirely happy with my next move, but finally decided to make it. I no longer thought I was taking over the initiative in this game, but at least I wanted there to be some imbalance, so that my opponent was not feeling too relaxed either.

17...e6!? There were all sorts of options here, but I finally settled on what looked the most logical, challenging White's pawn chain a little and creating further tension in the centre. The alternative was 17...♘xe2+ 18.♕xe2 ♗e5 19.♗f4 ♗xf4 20.♖xf4 e5!?, with

a highly unclear position. White has some avalanche potential on the kingside, but for now Black is in charge of the dark squares.

18.♘xd4!?

'Punishing' Black for not trading on e2. I was, in fact, slightly worried about this, but I still preferred to deal with this complex position rather than trading on e2 and leaving White with easy play.

18.♕d2 was normal as well, but I had expected the move in the game.

18...cxd4 19.♗f4

19...e5?!

Unfortunately, I played the text too quickly. Only when I started going further into the position on the next move, did I realize that I had missed an important resource.

19...♗e5 is arguably positionally desirable, but when you get mated, nobody will care how many dark squares you were controlling: 20.♗xe5 dxe5 21.f6!.

It's important to include 19...b3!: 20.cxb3 (20.♗xd6 is met by 20...♘a4! which, by the way, is not found so easily) 20...e5 21.♗d2 ♘a6. This is the position that I really wanted to get one move later in the game, but then it was too late. White may shut out the g7-bishop with g5-f6, but I felt I would in the meantime pick up the b3- and d3-pawns, more than compensating for the dead bishop. Also, philosophically speaking, the bishop is not exactly eternally buried on h8, since there can be a scenario in which Black eventually picks up the g5-pawn.

20.♗d2

Vladimir Fedoseev tries to fathom his opponent's intentions as Anish Giri strolls across the stage in Leiden's beautiful late-Gothic Pieterskerk, where Round 10 was played.

20...♗f6

Played with the intention of leaving the rook on f8 hanging after ♗h6. I wasn't too enthusiastic about the objective evaluation of the exchange sac, but between two options that I considered bad, I decided to choose the prettier one. There were two alternatives.

20...b3 21.g5 ♘a6 22.f6 bxc2 23.♕xc2 ♗h8 24.b4, and this I strongly disliked. As opposed to the situation in the 19...b3! variation, I don't control the b3-square and my knight doesn't have the perfect outpost on c5. Still, the position is actually unclear, but most players would find it hard to mentally deal with the h8-bishop.

20...♕h4 was kind of my plan A, but then I noticed that White has the nasty 21.♕c1! and I didn't see – or perhaps my subconscious didn't have

the guts to show me – 21...♗f6!, and the queen doesn't quite get trapped yet, although I wouldn't be feeling comfortable here.

21.♔h2?!

In itself this move is useful and all, but the fact that my opponent decided not to go for the exchange came as a pleasant surprise.

Stronger was 21.♗h6! g5 (21...♗g7 is what my opponent told me after the game. I have the feeling he may have missed 22.♕d2 ♕h4 23.♗g5!) 22.♗xf8. I was thinking for a very long time about how to arrange my pieces here and with what piece to recapture on f8. I believed that positionally this sac is reasonably sound, but the fact that the a-file is going to be controlled by White's rook was very concerning. I was trying to get some ...♗b5, ...♘a6-c5 set-up to work and also considering staying passive with ...♖b7 and trying to eventually get the knight to f6 via e8, but in none of the lines I was calculating did things work out the way I wanted them to. The main concern was that White would penetrate via the a-file, while unpleasant manoeuvres like ♕b1-a2 also came to mind.

Still, despite all this, I didn't dislike my position at all and that gave me quite some hope.

21...b3 I didn't make this move one move ago because of g5-f6, so here I decided it was time to make it. In fact, I was still underestimating 22.c3!.

22.♖a1?! After 22.c3! dxc3 23.bxc3 ♗a4, I think the game can still go very much either way, but the computer is convinced that White is doing very well and so be it: 24.♗h6 ♗g5 25.♗xf8 ♕xf8 26.♘e2 ♘a6 27.d4. I must say I do feel a little sad for my knight here, but Black is still in the game.

22...♗b5?! A little impulsive. Having played it, I regretted it badly, worried that ♖a7 would come, but fortunately my opponent passed on this opportunity as well.

23.♖a3?!
Not exerting much pressure. Now I can get on with my moves.
23.♖a7! actually works: 23...♘a6 24.fxg6 fxg6. Here it is pretty clear that while everything in my position is protected and covered, there is so much tension in the whole structure that one proper push in the right place would make it shake. To be honest, neither I nor my opponent saw this clearly, but the way is: 25.g5! bxc2 and now 26.♕g4! ♗g7 27.♖xf8+ ♕xf8, and here the point of the whole intro: 28.♘f5! gxf5 29.exf5, and White rolls, despite the c2-pawn being so close to the desired promotion square.

23...bxc2 24.♕xc2 ♘a6 25.b4 ♗g5

At first I was completely confused, thinking I must be taking over, but after a while my optimism diminished. It is not clear what to do here.
26.♖f3 ♖b6 27.♕a2
There is no clear threat, although White will try to destabilize my queenside somewhat with ♖a5 and then, after ...♘c7, with ♖a7. At the same time, I was thinking of ...h6 followed by ...♗xd2 and ...♕g5, but here I would first need to spend a tempo on ...♔g7. While all these slow lines seemed playable, I decided to use a tactical opportunity that presented itself:
27...♗f4!?
Besides 27...♔g7!?, with the idea of ...h6, there was also the simple 27...♗xd2!? 28.♕xd2 ♕h4!. Both were objectively better than the rather dubious move in the game.

28.♗xf4
My opponent goes for the most natural sequence, but I had expected 28.♖a5 (actually, 28.♖xf4! was strong) and now I was very tempted to sac a piece on d3 (which explains perhaps my decision to do a similar thing later on in the game). However, most likely I would have just made some normal move instead, as the sac looked too speculative. I would get some dark squares and a few easy moves, but potentially I could just end up in a lost position before I knew it: 28...♗xd3?! 29.♖xd3 ♘xb4 30.♗xb4 ♖xb4 31.♖aa3.
28...exf4

29.♘e2
My opponent must have underestimated my 30th move, else he would have gone for rook captures.
29.♖xf4! looks much less attractive, but actually it is stronger than the text: 29...♘xb4 30.♕d2. Now there is no ...d5, but there is 30...♕g5 and here the prosaic 31.♖f2 ♕xd2 32.♖xd2 leaves White with a slightly better endgame. On paper he has the 'bad' bishop, but Black actually has a weak d4-pawn and White's space on the kingside is beneficial.

29...♘xb4 30.♕d2 d5!
Without this push, White would definitely be happy with the latest transformations.

31.♘xf4!?
Played after quite some thought. Actually, I was extremely surprised to see the amount of ambition in my opponent, after he had, at least according to my estimation, missed my previous move, which was not only surprising but also strong.
As my opponent was thinking, the smoke cleared in my head and I saw that the best White can do is simply take the knight, after which, one way or the other, we will get a completely simplified position: 31.♕xb4 ♗xd3 32.♕xd4 ♗xe2 33.♖xf4 dxe4, and it will soon be time to shake hands.

31...♘xd3!?
I didn't think I was better after the long sequence starting with 31...dxe4, while here it was clear to me that, although I am probably not better, I felt my opponent's task of consolidating would be somewhat harder. The computer (as always correctly) disagrees.

32.♘xd5?! After 32.♖axd3 ♗xd3

Before the round in Leiden the Masters posed for a group portrait.
Magnus Carlsen needed no exhortation and went straight for the pulpit.

33.♕xd3 dxe4 34.♕xe4 ♖e8 35.♕d5 both 35...♕b8 or 35...♕c7 looked very promising and risk-free for me, but while I was probably right about the risk-free part, Black is definitely not better here. White will just reply ♔g1 and ♗f1 and be very safe. Black should probably go for an endgame, trade some kingside pawns and settle for a draw.

32...♕d6+ 33.♖g3 ♕xa3 34.♘xb6 ♕d6 35.♘d5?
A bit of a shocker, but my opponent played this move on autopilot. It seemed that by this point, the constant tension of the game got to him and he had a concentration lapse. 35.♕a5! was absolutely called for and in fact the move I expected. Now Black has to be precise to pose real problems: 35...♕e5! 36.♗f1 ♗c6! (an important finesse which is not easy to see) 37.♘c4 (White can probably defend after 37.♕xe5 ♘xe5 38.♘c4 ♘xc4 39.♗xc4 ♗xe4 40.♗d3, but there are no guarantees) 37...♕xe4

38.♗g2 ♕e2 39.♕d2 ♕xd2 40.♘xd2 ♘e5 41.♗xc6 ♘xc6 42.fxg6 hxg6 43.♖b3, and this endgame a pawn down should objectively still be within the drawing margins for White. A lot of hard work ahead, though.

35...♗c4!
A good move, after which White is suddenly lost. The knight on d5 is kind of dominated right there in the centre of the board and there is no stopping ...♗xd5, when all White will have left is an over-extended kingside with a bunch of weaknesses.

In a moment of chess blindness, Sam Shankland made one of the most painful mistakes possible, as he resigned in a position that his opponent could never win.

half a point ahead of Nepomniachtchi, Anand and Ding Liren. With Giri-Carlsen still on the menu, all eyes were on these two again. The tension only grew when, in Round 11, Giri caught up with the leader in a way that will not easily be forgotten. While Radjabov used the white pieces to draw against Carlsen, Giri was gifted the full point thanks to a hallucination of Sam Shankland, as well as to a little bit of psychological play by the Dutchman, who had read the American's body language and understood that he thought he was lost.

From an equal position, Shankland had drifted into an endgame that looked worrying, but in actual fact it was just a draw. Realizing this, Giri pushed 45.b6 and waited for his opponent's reaction.

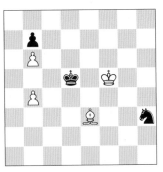

Giri-Shankland
Wijk aan Zee (11)
position after 45.b6

36.f6

36.g5 ♗xd5 37.♕xd3 ♗a8 is also lost, though in the game my bishop has an even better outpost, so practically speaking this was probably a better shot.

36.♕a5 is the most confusing and maybe the best defensive attempt. After let's say 36...♖b8, Black's position looks great and, according to my computer, is also objectively winning.

36...♗xd5 37.♕xd3

37.exd5 can be met trivially with 37...♘f4!, when White is dead lost, as 38.♕xd4 is met by 38...♘e2.

37...♗e6

Even better than 37...♗a8. White's position is hopeless; the threat of ♕d2-h6 can be easily parried, since the f6-pawn needs defending. Now things ended swiftly.

38.♔g1 ♗c4!

Winning pretty much by force.

39.♕f3 d3 40.e5 ♕xe5 41.♕e3 ♖e8

White will lose a full bishop in the ensuing endgame, so my opponent resigned.

■ ■ ■

And so, three rounds before the end, Carlsen was leading by half a point, followed by Giri, who in his turn was

He had guessed right, because Black resigned. Shankland was under the impression that he had to get his king to a8 to make a draw and didn't see how he could get there, but in fact getting his king to c8 (so 45...♔d6) would have sufficed. Just try it out for yourself – there is no way that White can expel the black king and win after capturing the black knight. As Giri put it, 'The only way I can win this is if he resigns, otherwise there is no way I can break through.' To which he added tongue-in-cheek, 'Maybe Magnus Carlsen could, but I can't.'

The only slight doubt Giri had was whether Shankland had really resigned. So he asked him, and when he got confirmation, he knew that he had caught up with Carlsen. For the American it was obviously a very unfortunate moment and one that cannot really be explained. As you could read everywhere, the entire world – once they had consulted their engines – except for him had seen that it was a draw. Of course, Shankland did the only thing he could do. The next day he won a fine game against Nepomniachtchi.

The decisive game

Giri's luck didn't end here. The next day he ended up in a really difficult position against Radjabov, which objectively speaking might have been lost. Again he resorted to psychology, offering a draw in the hope that his opponent was not entirely sure of his chances. Radjabov did indeed hesitate, suddenly started seeing all kinds of ghosts, and ended up taking the draw.

With this draw Giri limited the damage in the fight for first place, since Magnus Carlsen won a good game against Jan-Krzysztof Duda, a game that, in hindsight, decided the tournament in Carlsen's favour.

NOTES BY
Peter Heine Nielsen

Magnus Carlsen
Jan-Krzysztof Duda
Wijk aan Zee 2019 (12)
Queen's Gambit Declined, Vienna Variation

1.d4 ♘f6 2.c4 e6 3.♘f3 d5 4.♘c3 dxc4
Duda stays loyal to his tournament preparation. The Vienna had netted him two effortless draws already.
5.e4 ♗b4 6.♗xc4!?
In the first round, Vidit played the traditional 6.♗g5, after which Duda surprised with 6...b5!? 7.a4 c5. Magnus follows Duda's game against Mamedyarov, in which White played the now popular pure pawn sacrifice, aiming for quick development.
6...♘xe4 7.0-0

7...♘f6!?
7...♗xc3 8.bxc3 ♘xc3 gives Black even two extra pawns, but the white initiative becomes overwhelming. Danish IM Steffen Pedersen and Swedish GM Tiger Hillarp Persson showed me this idea way before it became popular, and I managed to win a blitz game against Van Wely in the German Team Championship before forgetting about it. And then being completely lost against Pedersen himself in a blindfold event in Denmark in 2007 that was won by Magnus himself, as it was organized in order to give him training for his first appearance in the Melody Amber tournament.
The basic tactical point was 9.♕b3 ♘d5 10.♗a3 ♘c6 11.♖fe1 ♘ce7 12.♗xe7 ♘xe7 13.d5 exd5 14.♗xd5 0-0 15.♗xf7+! ♖xf7 16.♖ad1 ♕f8 17.♘g5, and this was also my game against Pedersen.
8.♕a4+ ♘c6 9.♘e5 ♖b8

Obviously, the line has evolved, and Black has found more sensible solutions than the greedy early attempts. 9...♖b8 was Caruana's choice against Aronian from the Norway Chess tournament in 2018, and obviously

part of the American's preparation for that year's Candidates Tournament. Funnily enough, it had already been played by Magnus's second Laurent Fressinet against Halkias in 2010, when Fressinet's loss had nothing to do with his position after the opening.
10.♖d1!? Aronian took on c6, and Halkias played 10.d5. Magnus plays a less direct approach, but blitzed out the following moves as he was obvi-

> **'Duda knew the risk he was taking, but the young Pole showed numerous times in Wijk that he is not afraid of a challenge.'**

ously still in his preparation. Duda knew the risk he was taking. In hindsight, playing Caruana's favourite line, which Magnus obviously must have prepared, might seem like a bad idea, but the young Pole showed numerous times in Wijk that he is not afraid of a challenge.
10...0-0 11.♘xc6 bxc6 12.♕xa7
Quite a typical scenario in modern chess. White threatened a blitz attack by sacrificing a pawn, Black chose a solid continuation, and suddenly White changes gears and is now playing for a better pawn structure and a potentially passed a-pawn.

12...♗d7

Threatening a 'perpetual' against White's queen with ...♖a8 and ...♖b8.
13.♕a4 c5 14.♕c2
This is why White included 10.♖d1 0-0. He needed the rook to protect the d4-pawn.
14...cxd4 15.♖xd4 ♗c5?!
In a video interview after the tournament Magnus mentioned that he recalled asking some of his seconds trying to sell him on to this concept: 'Why can Black not just go 15...♗c5, followed by 16...h6? Somebody switched on the engine, and said 17.♗xh6 and 18.♕d2 is +1. But no one told me what this +1 consisted of.'

16.♖h4!? It was noteworthy that the Norwegian supercomputer Sesse preferred 16.♖d1, aiming for more positional methods.
16...h6? Played quickly, but walking straight into White's preparation. Or at least sort of preparation.
17.♗xh6!

17...gxh6 18.♕d2
Black's problem is that h6 cannot be protected, and losing the pawn basically leads to mate on h8. 18...h5 19.♕g5+ ♔h8 20.♘e4! also causes the game to end immediately, so Black

has to call himself lucky that things are actually not worse than they are.
18...♘h7! Or 18...♘e8, leading to the same thing.
19.♕xh6

19...♗xf2+! Black sacrifices the bishop to force a queen swap. White cannot decline with 20.♔h1, since the bishop on f2 is also threatening the white rook on h4.
20.♔xf2 ♕f6+ 21.♕xf6 ♖xb2+!
Not only does Black have a saving check forcing off the queens, he even manages to pick up a pawn with this intermezzo, levelling the material balance.
22.♔g1 ♘xf6 23.♖f1!
Maybe this position does not really show it, but White's initiative is still very threatening. Since Magnus knew the machines evaluated the sacrifice on h6 as advantageous for White, and (correctly) saw no better option than this, it meant he could enter this seemingly innocent position with confidence.

23...♔g7!? Duda realized his problems and went for a practical solution. 23...♘e8 24.♖f3 f5 25.♖g3+ ♘g7 is the computer's preferred line,

but showing a considerable initiative for White after 26.♘e2, followed by 27.♘f4 or 27.♘d4.
24.♖f3 Black's problem is the safety of his king. 25.♖g3+, basically mating, is the immediate threat.
24...♖g8

25.♖hf4! Black's last move has the dual purpose of providing an escape route via f8 for the king, as well as attacking g2 with the rook. White, however, is just in time to start his own attack on the f-file and Duda is now forced to give up material.
25...♗c6 26.♖xf6!
If 26.♖g3+?! ♔f8 27.♖xf6, Black has 27...♖xg3 28.hxg3 ♖xg2+, followed by 29...♖c2, winning back the piece.
26...♗xf3 27.♖xf3 ♖d8
White has two minor pieces for the rook, but the reduced remaining material and Black's activity makes it a kind of 50-50 bet whether Black will manage to hold the draw.
28.♖f2 ♖b4

29.♗b5?!
Too ambitious. More stable was 29.♗b3, but Magnus had underestimated Black's strong resource on move 30.

29...♖a8 30.a4 c6!

Due to 31.♗xc6 ♖c8!, winning a piece, Duda now manages to push White's bishop away from b5, which means that the knight is forced to stay on c3 to defend the pawn on a4.

31.♗e2 ♖a5 32.♖f3 f5 33.♔f2 ♖c5 34.♗d1

Defending the pawn on a4 and relieving the knight on c3 of its defensive duties.

For the 'On Tour rounds', Magnus Carlsen and his second Peter Heine Nielsen had a comfortable Jaguar and driver at their disposal.

34...e5?!

Logical. Advancing the pawn while exploiting that 35.♖xf5 can be met by 35...♖xc3. However, it does weaken the f5-pawn, meaning that Black will have to advance it further and thus allow White's knight to permanently settle on f4.

35.♘e2 ♔f6 36.♖a3 ♖b1

37.♔e1!

A good retreat, defending the d1-bishop and not fearing 37...♖cd5 in view of 38.♘c3!, forking the black rooks.

37...e4 38.g3!

Not falling for the trick 38.a5? ♖bb5! 39.a6 ♖a5!, winning the white a-pawn.

38...♔e5 39.h4 ♖a5 40.h5 c5

41.♔d2 c4 42.♔c2 ♖b8 43.♔c3 ♖b1 44.♔c2 ♖b8 45.♔c1 ♖b6 46.♗c2 ♖d6 47.♘f4

White's pieces start landing on their ideal squares, but even so breaking Black's resistance is not at all easy.

47...♖c5 48.♖e3 ♔d4 49.♖e1

49...♖h6?!

Duda did not realize that this was a crucial moment of the game, and just played a common-sense move.

He had his chance, since 49...♔c3! would have ensured counterplay sufficient for serious drawing chances, because after 50.♘e2+ ♔b4 Black makes it much more difficult for White to improve his position than in the game.

50.♔d2! A very strong move, either luring Black's pawn to c3, when b3 becomes available for the white bishop, or, as in the game, getting White's king to c3.

50...♖e5 51.♘e2+ ♔c5

52.♖h1!

'Given the significance of the tournament for the coastal village, it would be befitting if one day there would be a real Magnus Carlsen street.'

Covering the h5-pawn and getting ready for ♔c3. Black can stop this with 52...♔b4, but then 53.♔e3!, intending ♔d4 and ♖b1+, will be decisive.

52...♖e8 53.♔c3 ♖g8 54.♖b1! ♖xh5 55.♗xe4! ♖e8

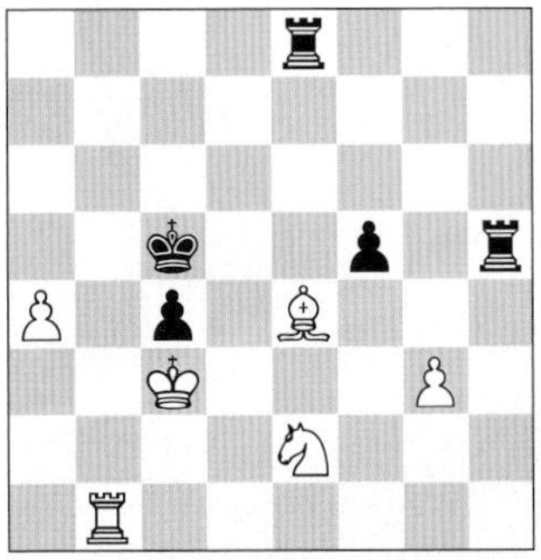

56.♘f4! A fascinating tactical sequence, despite the limited amount of material. Its end result is just the elimination of the kingside pawns.

56...♖g5 57.♖b5+ ♔d6 58.♗xf5 ♖xg3+ 59.♔d4!?

Taking on c4 was also possible, but Magnus's idea with the previous moves was aiming exactly for this position. Material has been reduced even further, but Black's king suddenly and surprisingly finds itself under a devastating attack!

59...♖g1 60.♖b6+

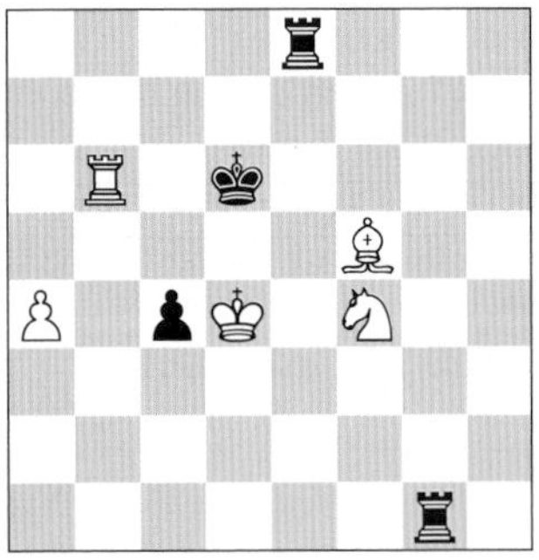

60...♔e7! The good thing from Black's perspective is that he avoids getting mated. The problem is that the king ends up too far away from a8.

61.♘g6+ ♔f7 62.♘e5+ ♔g8 63.♘xc4 Materialistic, at last.

63...♖a8 64.a5 ♖a1 65.♖b5 ♖a7 66.♗e4 ♖c7 67.♖f5 ♔g7 68.♗c2 ♖c1 69.♔c3 ♖f7 70.♖xf7+! ♔xf7

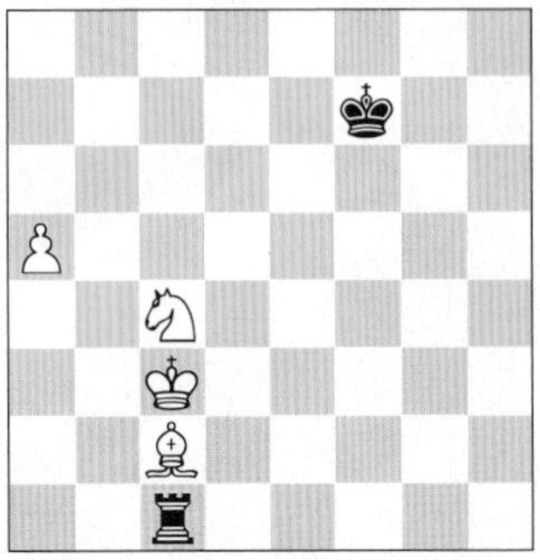

An interesting observation was made by the spectators following the game in the live chat. This ending is generally a draw, as proven by the tablebases. Here, however, the black king is not close enough to a7, and with his next move Magnus shuts down any black hope of stopping the a-pawn with his rook from a1.

71.♘a3! Now White's a-pawn queens trivially. Not wanting the World Champion to end the game by showing his skills of mating with knight and bishop, Duda resigned.

Street name

As Giri had foreseen (or hoped) at the opening ceremony, his last-round game against Carlsen would decide the winner. But he needed a win, and how realistic was that? Would he be able to find a crack in the armour that Carlsen had moulded so meticulously for his match against Caruana?

In the end, Giri also decided to take on the Sveshnikov, but he didn't achieve anything and even got into trouble (see Jan Timman's column). Luckily, his psychological insight again came to the rescue when he offered a draw, sensing that Carlsen was happy to call it a day. On the strength of this draw, Giri finished clear second, an excellent result that made him move up one slot in the world rankings, to fourth place. For Carlsen it meant his seventh victory in Wijk aan Zee, a very impressive achievement. He made his debut in the Masters in 2007, when he was 16, and scored his first win when he was 17. During this year's tournament, several streets in Wijk aan Zee were temporarily named after chess players. Given the significance of the tournament for the coastal village, it would be befitting if one day there would be a real Magnus Carlsen street. ■

Wijk aan Zee 2019 – Masters **cat. XXI**

					1	2	3	4	5	6	7	8	9	10	11	12	13	14		TPR
1	Magnus Carlsen	IGM	NOR	2835	*	½	½	½	1	½	½	½	1	1	½	1	1	½	9	2887
2	Anish Giri	IGM	NED	2783	½	*	0	½	½	½	½	1	1	1	1	½	½	1	8½	2860
3	Ian Nepomniachtchi	IGM	RUS	2763	½	1	*	½	½	1	½	0	½	½	1	½	0	1	7½	2809
4	Ding Liren	IGM	CHN	2813	½	½	½	*	½	½	½	1	½	½	½	½	1	½	7½	2805
5	Vishy Anand	IGM	IND	2773	0	½	½	½	*	½	½	½	½	½	½	1	1	1	7½	2808
6	Vidit Gujrathi	IGM	IND	2695	½	½	0	½	½	*	0	½	½	½	½	1	1	1	7	2786
7	Teimour Radjabov	IGM	AZE	2757	½	½	½	½	½	1	*	½	½	½	0	½	½	½	6½	2752
8	Samuel Shankland	IGM	USA	2725	½	0	1	0	½	½	½	*	½	½	0	½	1	1	6½	2755
9	Richard Rapport	IGM	HUN	2731	0	0	½	½	½	½	½	½	*	1	½	½	1	½	6½	2754
10	Jan-Krzysztof Duda	IGM	POL	2738	0	0	½	½	½	½	½	½	0	*	1	½	0	1	5½	2697
11	Vladimir Fedoseev	IGM	RUS	2724	½	0	0	½	½	½	1	1	½	0	*	½	0	0	5	2668
12	Shakhriyar Mamedyarov	IGM	AZE	2817	0	½	½	½	0	0	½	½	½	½	½	*	½	½	5	2661
13	Jorden van Foreest	IGM	NED	2612	0	½	1	0	0	0	½	0	0	1	1	½	*	0	4½	2653
14	Vladimir Kramnik	IGM	RUS	2777	½	0	0	½	0	0	½	0	½	0	1	½	1	*	4½	2641

Emanuel Lasker: 'By some ardent enthusiasts Chess has been elevated into a science or an art. It is neither; but its principal characteristic seems to be – what human nature mostly delights in – a fight.'

Matt Goss: 'This is my cave area. I have crystals everywhere. Love a bit of chess, have a few glasses of scotch, have a long game of chess.' *(The late 1980s frontman of English band Bros, in the new cult documentary 'Bros: After the Screaming Stops')*

Vladimir Kramnik: 'I really can't remember what my current rating is. I wouldn't like to sound immodest, but when you become World Champion, you don't pay too much attention to ratings anymore.'

David Shenk: 'I was obsessed with this question of how chess could endure for so many centuries and across so many societies, remaining popular in literally all age groups. (..) Aside from chess and beer, it's almost impossible to find common things that stretch across such large historical spans.' *(The author of 'The Immortal Game', explaining what motivated him to write his book)*

Kevin McKenna: 'In post-Reformation Scotland Mary was reviled for her Catholic faith and for her sexual allure at a time when princesses were considered mere chattels and chess pieces to be paraded across the chessboard kingdoms of Europe to seal treaties and unite empires.' *(The former deputy editor of The Herald and executive editor of the Daily Mail in Scotland, writing in The Guardian on the new movie 'Mary Queen of Scots', starring Saoirse Ronan)*

Timur Gareyev: 'It's like painting where you're continuously doing something, you're immersing yourself in that moment, and you become that brush, become that paint, so here you become the chess pieces.' *(The Uzbeki-born US GM, explaining how he clears his mind during his blindfold feats)*

Pal Benko: 'In the Soviets' view, chess was not merely an art or a science or even a sport; it was what it had been invented to simulate: war.'

Yuri Averbakh: 'It is impossible to ignore a highly important factor of the chess struggle – psychology.' *(The world's oldest-living GM, who on 8 February turned 97)*

Adhiban Baskaran: 'After every loss, I ask myself – is this defeat going to stop me? And the answer is always NO! So, I get back on my feet and get back to work!'

Lewis Goodall: 'Brexit is a game of three dimensional political chess – and Jeremy Corbyn has made his biggest move yet.' *(The Sky News political correspondent goes overboard on the chess metaphors game for Brexit, as the Labour leader adds a strategic late move in the process in early February)*

Jon Manley: 'James Mason died on this day in 1905. I once spent a soggy Sunday afternoon seeking his grave in an Essex churchyard. "Not one of my better dates," recalls my then-girlfriend.' *(The Kingpin editor's tweet on the 12 January anniversary death date of the mid-19th century Irish-born master)*

Bill Nack: 'He looked deeper into a race than anybody else, analysing horses and jockeys, and out there he was always thinking one or two strides ahead of everyone around him. Bailey saw a horse race as Bobby Fischer saw a game of speed-chess — as a series of rapid calculations leading to a foreseeable, logical conclusion.' *(The renowned Sports Illustrated feature writer profiling in 2006 the success of top US jockey, Jerry Bailey)*

Hein Donner: 'What's this? Are you teaching the poor thing to play chess? Fie, for shame! Why not have him drink hard liquor or take him off to a brothel, while you're at it!' *(The Dutch GM and chess writer on teaching chess to a child)*

Interview Vladimir Kramnik

'I never tried to compete with others, I always competed with myself.'

Two days after the Tata Steel tournament, Vladimir Kramnik announced his retirement from professional chess at the age of 43. His decision elicited reactions of shock, sympathy and admiration from all around the globe. **DIRK JAN TEN GEUZENDAM** visited the 14th World Champion at his home in Geneva for a frank and revealing interview about authenticity, ambition and much more.
'I don't understand how I could become World Champion. Usually champions want to win. For me winning was never the major motivation.'

O n January 29, close to lunchtime, a limousine drops off Vladimir Kramnik in the historic centre of The Hague. Later that day, he will give the traditional 'post-Wijk aan Zee' Tata Steel simul in the Dutch parliament. But first, he had said, he wanted to have a quiet lunch and 'see the Rembrandts' in the Mauritshuis, one of the richest collections of 17th-century Dutch paintings at a stone's throw from the parliament.

As he arrives at my home, he holds up his telephone and suggests: 'Maybe you can check the first sentence; see if it's OK.' Slightly puzzled I have a look, get what feels like a punch in my stomach and understand that today is going to be very different from what we had planned. On the screen I read the first sentence of a press release announcing his retirement from professional chess, a message that soon will be shared with the world.

We did go to see the Rembrandts and we did have lunch, but it had all become background. From the moment the news is released, his telephone keeps buzzing and beeping. Not suppressing his curiosity, he looks at all the messages and the numbers that try to reach him, but only sends brief replies to a few – probably mainly emoticons, of which he is unashamedly fond. One of the first colleagues to react is Vishy Anand, which brings a broad smile to his face.

In between he tries to explain what has led him to his decision. 'I began to feel that I could no longer give it my all. Maybe the last tournament where I did so was the Candidates tournament in Berlin. After that, with every tournament, with every month... I come to play chess, I want to, but I cannot force myself to make an effort. In Wijk aan Zee, I had already decided to quit and then I sit there and I know I have to calculate a variation. And I want to, but I cannot force myself to. I feel that

Vladimir Kramnik with his wife Marie-Laure and their daughter Daria and son Vadim at their home in Geneva.

it not only doesn't make sense, but that you're also betraying chess and yourself. If I keep on playing like this, I am just wasting time.

'I told Evgeny Bareev, a friend of mine, that I was losing interest and that I would probably quit, and he said he knew the feeling. He said that for him enjoying to play chess is very much connected with quality. The quality that is satisfactory to you. He said, "For the chess that I produce now, I don't have to be Bareev. Any guy in an open tournament can do this." For me it was not only this. It was like a chain reaction. You don't play well because there's not enough motivation, there's not enough motivation because you cannot force yourself... Finally my decision was purely intuitional, like I always played chess. It doesn't fit me anymore, I want to go and do something else. It may be socially less prestigious, but it will be new and I will be able to improve.'

Shelves full of trophies

The rest of the afternoon left little time to continue our talk, and so, two weeks later, I arrive in Geneva to look back on one of the most impressive careers in modern chess. Vladimir Kramnik, his wife Marie-Laure and their children Daria (10) and Vadim (6) live in a stately apartment building in a peaceful residential area only a couple of hundred metres away from Geneva's main shopping street and the lake. It's easy to understand that they were attracted by the light and the high ceilings in the apartment when they moved here from Paris in 2014. At the back, overlooking a garden, Vladimir has his study, where the shelves are filled with books and trophies – many big ones that bring back memories of triumphs in Linares, Monaco, Dortmund or his match against Leko in Brissago, but also two Chess Oscars and an impressive troll, which used to frighten Daria but now amuses her, for his win in the Troll Masters in Gausdal back in 1992.

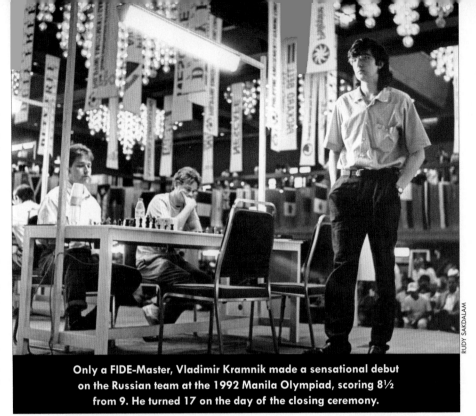

Only a FIDE-Master, Vladimir Kramnik made a sensational debut on the Russian team at the 1992 Manila Olympiad, scoring 8½ from 9. He turned 17 on the day of the closing ceremony.

The main trophy, for his win in the World Championship match against Garry Kasparov in 2000, sits on the mantelpiece over the fireplace in the living room. It occupies a special place, but apparently it has not been polished for quite some years. Years after the match, a friend of Kramnik's bought it from match organizer Raymond Keene and gave it to the winner of the match, believing he was the rightful owner.

However, the real eye-catcher in the living-room is a colourfully painted Erard grand piano that Marie-Laure bought when she was still a journalist for the French daily *Le Figaro*. She tells me that the Erard dates back to 1896 and that Debussy played on it.

Vladimir Kramnik always felt at home in artistic circles, which, with his family background, cannot come as a real surprise. As we sit down for our talk in a café across the street, I ask him how he thinks growing up in an artistic family influenced his chess career.

'My mother taught music at the conservatory and at our local music school. With only 70,000 inhabitants, Tuapse, where I was born, was a provincial place by Soviet standards, but they had a huge four-storied music school. In the weekends she rehearsed at home. She liked Chopin very much and a couple of Chopin etudes I still cannot listen to, because she would repeat some parts endlessly. Since it was only a 30-square-metre apartment, you would hear it all the time. If I hear those pieces, I immediately switch off the music; it's like water dripping from a tap.

'My father was mainly a sculptor, but he also painted. He liked to make copies of famous paintings. We had a copy of Kramskoi's *Portrait of an Unknown Woman* in our home, and my brother and I had a copy of a Rembrandt painting in our room. I was often in my father's study, where he had a lot of art books, some two or three thousand. He was earning very well, three or four times the average salary. But there was no way to spend this money, so he bought all these books, because he loved art.

'My mother taught me to play the piano a bit, but I was more interested in chess. Actually, I liked drawing, and I once asked my father to teach me, but I am so ungifted in this, I simply cannot draw a straight line, and soon I gave up.

'I suppose my background had a serious impact, but you don't know in what way. And actually chess, from the very beginning, when my father taught me, when I was five or six, it caught me, I don't know why. Chess just found me. It was a very fortunate meeting. I asked my father to buy me some books and I would just analyse on my own. That's strange, usually kids like to play, but I was immediately very much into work. It just happened naturally. It is often said that you need a certain level, 2000 or something, to appreciate the richness of chess or the aesthetic pleasure of certain positions, but I had this from the beginning. I was especially keen on endgames, which is usually not something kids like. I enjoyed delicate endgame techniques no less than beautiful combinations.'

In an interview in 2004, after the match against Leko, you famously said, 'A painter never asks people what they want to see. He paints.' This was in defence of your style, which was criticized at the time. I thought that comparison was not coincidental.
'Definitely not. One thing I am happy with is that from my childhood on, I always did things the way I wanted to do them. The influence of the outside world was always limited. In my philosophy it was very important not to become a tool or slave. Society

'When I was five or six, it caught me, I don't know why. Chess just found me. It was a very fortunate meeting.'

is watching you and you have to give what they want. If I was selling fruit, I would try to find the best fruit for my customers, but since I am doing something in sport, art, I will do it the way I want. I believe that everyone should try to be authentic and personal, and then, if someone likes it, fine; if they don't, also fine. This may sound arrogant, but it's not, it's in fact the only honest way to exist. Once you do something creative, it's simply insincere if you start thinking about how people will perceive it. I can assure you that painters who had a huge impact were not interested if people liked their work or not. Van Gogh thought he was not a great painter, as he wrote in many letters to his brother. He wrote that he could never do what these impressionists were doing; they were way above him. He was just doing sincerely what he did and he became maybe the most influential painter of that time.'

Like many painters, you had different periods in your career. Periods when your play was more positional, or more aggressive. How do you remember the Kramnik who made his breakthrough at the Manila Olympiad – the artist as a young man?
'I had a lot of energy and drive. After I had finished school, when I was 17, I moved to Moscow to live there alone. I had already been travelling alone a lot, but this was a kind of new freedom, when you are no longer told what to do and what not to do, and I was feeling so good inside, I was so happy. Not because I didn't like it at home, but it was a new life. I was free and my chess was reflecting it. Free to play the way I felt like, a kind of happy chess.

'All the different periods I had always reflected my state of mind. Sometimes it's difficult to formulate this, but that first period was very clear. I remember the way I felt and I am not sure I will ever feel the same, because I was just enjoying every minute of the day. Between tournaments, I would stay in a hotel in Moscow; it was cheap at that time. I would work on chess, see friends sometimes, I was happy every minute! This releases a lot of creative energy and I started to win everything. And I was absolutely surprised myself, all the time. What's going on? I was never over-confident. I never thought I'd achieve what I achieved, not even close. Why did they include me in the Russian team for the Manila Olympiad? Most probably I will fail. And then I had this result. How come? I always had this feeling of amazement.'

You were also exploring other sides of life. I remember a story from the French league, where you had cognac at lunch before the game...
'(Apparently for him it triggers a different memory) This was in Amsterdam, the 1993 VSB tournament, in the press centre. I won the first round against Nigel (Short), which was a big success, and we started analysing. One of the organizers asked me what I wanted to drink. And I said, maybe a cognac, and then another. And then they put a bottle, especially for me, in this hospitality room.

'In fact, I have to confess that a couple of times I tried to drink before the game, but just as an experiment. But I didn't like the effect. Sometimes I felt sleepy, so I decided this was not my cup of tea. So only after the game. These decisions were always intuitive. Not like, now I want to drink or now I won't drink during this tournament. At some point, I started feeling that I was not enjoying it anymore. There was no clear goal or reasoning. I drank quite a bit until the age of 23, and then I did it occasionally, but it was not giving me enough pleasure and at some point I more or less stopped. Very simple, no special reasons.'

Which were the periods when you felt you were playing your best chess?
'There were a few periods of one or two years that I was playing really well. Somewhere around 1997, 98. And of course 1992 in its own way.

Vladimir Kramnik

Born: June 25, 1975, Tuapse, Soviet Union

Career highlights

1992	Dortmund Open, 1st
1992	Manila Olympiad, 8½/9, gold medal best performance (2958)
1995	Wins 'Dortmund' for the first time
1995	Horgen, 1=
1995	Belgrade 1=
1996	January, 1st in world rankings
1996	Wins 'Monaco' for the first time
2000	Linares, shared first with Kasparov
2000	London, beats Kasparov in World Championship match, 8½-6½
2001	Wins 'Dortmund' for the 6th time
2004	Linares, 1st
2004	Brissago, World Championship match vs Leko, 7-7, keeps title
2006	Turin Olympiad, gold medal best performance (2847)
2006	Elista, World Championship match, defeats Topalov in playoff
2007	Wins 'Monaco' for the 6th time
2007	Moscow, Tal Memorial, 1st
2009	Moscow, Tal Memorial, 1st
2010	Bilbao Grand Slam Final, 1st
2011	Wins 'Dortmund' for the 10th time
2011	London Chess Classic, 1st
2013	Tromsø, World Cup, 1st
2017	July, 2nd in world rankings

Then definitely 2000, 2001. Because people often forget that in 2001, after the match against Kasparov, I had some other fantastic results. Then I had this break, more or less, when all these problems started. Then definitely 2006, 2007. And maybe 2013, when I won the World Cup and almost qualified from the Candidates tournament. And maybe 2017, when I got second in the world again.'

When you were at your best, you were often seen as a standard, almost a standard of perfection.
'No, no. Every player when he is at his

'I was trying to take the best of everyone without trying to copy them. Even at the age of seven I never tried to copy anyone.'

best is unbeatable. You have to have a certain level, of course, but you don't need to be a genius like Garry. Take Topalov. I don't compare him to Garry, but when he was at his best he was really extremely strong.'

One of the nicest tributes after you announced your retirement was the mock cover of Now In Chess that revealed that AlphaZero is Vladimir Kramnik...
'(Laughs). I didn't see that one. You see, I never looked at myself and I still don't... thinking about my impact on the game. I find it too narcissistic. I just do, I paint (laughs), that's all – I do, I don't assess. I was never too happy with what I did; I always thought I should do better. But what I do think is that I was always authentic. I played chess, worked on chess, basically for the sake of it. I like the process in itself. I was doing it with my heart. Sometimes I managed, sometimes not.'

Over these, say, 25 years, your taste must have changed and developed. Are the players that you admire now different from your early inspirers?
'Yes, this changes, but that doesn't mean that in three years it cannot be totally different again. It's a process. As wise people tell us, the only constant in our lives is change. But I never had idols or favourite players. I liked Alekhine, Karpov, Kasparov, but I was trying to take the best of everyone and trying to understand what that was, without trying to copy them. It's strange, but even at the age of seven I never tried to copy anyone. Somehow I was just playing my own game.

'What I like in chess is if there is a certain concept behind it, a vision of what you do. You play chess and you're not making moves to make

a point but to play chess. And chess represents something that you believe in. You can also see it in some young players, although the use of the computer has led to a certain levelling of style. Magnus definitely plays his chess with his vision, taking it as a whole. His chess is authentic, it's global, a vision of the game. Aronian definitely has his own style, too. But I don't want to name names, then someone will be forgotten...'

Irrespective of your chess philosophy and your wish for authenticity, you also had to compete. What was it that made you fight?
'Actually, I was thinking about that not that long ago. When I started thinking about retiring, I wondered why I lost this drive, this motivation. And I began to dig deep. I am actually not a competitive person by nature, which is all very strange.

The mock cover of 'Now In Chess' that 'revealed the AlphaZero prank'.

I don't understand how I could become World Champion. Usually champions want to win. For me, winning was never the major motivation. The major motivation was an introverted challenge. I always liked to improve. In chess and also in life. I always wanted to improve, to play better. Becoming World Champion was a clear sign that it had happened, but the feeling inside that I was playing better was always my driving force. It's quite a miracle to me how I could win so much without this competitive drive. This wish to always get better must have been very strong, this permanent inner challenge.

'I've understood this from my childhood, but when I saw this saying years ago, I understood that it was mine and I really deeply believe in it: The only person you have to compare yourself with is you from yesterday. I never tried to compare myself with people or compete with them; I always competed with myself. Tomorrow I want to be better than yesterday. It's very introverted, if not autistic, but that's how it is.'

The outside world could see how motivated you were by the sacrifices you made. Before the match against Kasparov you lost weight, 15 kilos, and quit smoking. Because you wanted it so badly.
'I can tell you honestly, even if people with a different mentality may not believe it, but I didn't care about winning the match. I didn't believe so much that I was going to win. That was not the point. The point was that I felt that this was the moment I was facing the biggest challenge you can have in chess against the best player of the day and one of the best in history, in a 16-game match, face to face, a litmus test. Of course I know that I am already a good player, but this is a mirror; it will show you who you are in chess. He could have crushed me, or I might have lost minus-2, it might be an equal fight, or

(whispers) even miraculously I could win. I didn't know and actually I didn't think about it. I only wanted to be ready for it and not think afterwards that I hadn't done enough. It was a once-in-a-lifetime experience, I had to be ready for it. I was at my best and I thought that if I lost, I just wasn't good enough.

'I could do this because I was playing Garry. When I played Shirov, I couldn't (referring to the match in 1998 that he lost and which earned Shirov the right to a match against Kasparov that never happened – DJtG). I knew that I could beat Shirov, but Kasparov... that I didn't know. I wanted to become World Champion, but that was not the goal.'

And the day after you won, you started smoking again.
'(Thinks back) After I won we had a serious party. (Starts laughing) Evgeny Bareev was in quite difficult shape. And not only he. It was clear to me that in this particular match I had not been worse. Maybe Kasparov was not in his best shape, but for me it was the end of a story. I had proven to myself that I could do this. I can beat a really great player. Not the end of the story, but the end of a big chapter. Now I felt I had nothing to prove anymore, to myself. What is next? To reach 2900? I was at a loss, and then I tried to change my style, my repertoire and it was not that successful. It was a combination of many things. Yes, also my health problems, but that was later. It started with chess politics, which influenced me really badly psychologically. It was this kind of period when you don't know what you want. Your life changes dramatically, you become a public person, people wanting you to do all kinds of things. It was a complete change. Before I was on

After they finished shared first in 2000, Garry Kasparov handed the traditional Linares trophy to Vladimir Kramnik, a generous gesture he may have regretted later that year when he lost the world title to his former pupil.

ROSA DE LAS NIEVES

my own. Living the life I wanted to live. With very few responsibilities. And since this was not what I liked, it was not a positive change. People who search for fame and glory, it gives them a lot of energy; for me it was the other way round. It was a big weight on my shoulders that I didn't manage to cope with in the right manner. I was not happy, the joy of daily life, of working on chess and playing tournaments was missing. And it began to be reflected in my chess. My play became dry and uninspired sometimes.'

Besides the Kasparov rivalry, there were others. How would you compare that rivalry with that which you had with Anand?
'Oh, that is totally different. With

Vishy it was a long rivalry of equals. We entered the chess scene more or less at the same time. Garry was a teacher, a god; there is no comparison. I didn't feel like Garry's rival; he had no rivals for quite a long period of time. I was the one who came closest, with Vishy. I was more competing with Vishy and Chuky (Ivanchuk) and others, not with Garry. Our real competition was not that long, unfortunately, from 2000 to 2004 or 2005, when he left. With Vishy it was all my life.'

When Kasparov quit, Anand said that one day it would start itching again and he might come back. Now Anand is saying more or less the same about you. It sounds as if he feels left alone.
'No, no matter if you have good relations or bad relations, it's part of your life. There's something emotional in it, as if some part of your life is over, some small part of you dies. For me coming back to chess at the moment

'I wanted to become World Champion, but that was not the goal.'

feels unrealistic. Life has taught me that anything can happen, but for the moment I would say there is practically no chance.'

There also was the rivalry with Magnus Carlsen. People speak with regret about the rematch with Kasparov that never took place. I think it was also a pity there was never a match between you and Magnus.
'I would have loved to play a match with Magnus. As I would have loved another match with Garry or with Vishy, but what happened, happened. There are a number of matches in the history of chess that everyone would have loved to see, such as Fischer-Kasparov, and they just never happened. That's life. I have played more than I could ever have imagined. I played against Garry, against Topalov, against Leko, against Anand. Even when I was already a professional, even when I was number 3 in the world, I could never have imagined I would have such a career. But it's true that there was a period when I thought about a match with Magnus. At some point, I started feeling that the only thing that could still force me to give it all was a match with Magnus. Even if it was not a world championship match, just as a challenge.'

For me, one of your most impressive achievements was winning the World Cup in Tromsø in 2013. As if in a trance, sticking to a boring, strict schedule, you seemed to pursue your goal with only one aim: a match against Magnus?
'No, no, there was no goal. There are periods when you feel well and everything fits together. When I came there, I had already qualified for the Candidates, but it was in the rules that to play in the Candidates, I had to take part in the World Cup. I left

Vladimir Kramnik with the Howard Staunton trophy, for his victory over Garry Kasparov. The precious sterling silver cup only reached him years later when a friend bought it for him from organizer Raymond Keene.

my family on holiday in France, and I told them I might come back in one week. I was ready to be knocked out, but I started feeling so good there. Because of the nature, the nice air. I was having two-hour walks every day, to Tromsø and back. I like this northern nature, much more than the south. Already after a few days I was feeling so much energy, was so happy to be there. So for me this boring routine was not boring at all. I was happy to play, but I was not determined to win.'

Let's talk about a disappointment then. At the 2013 London Candidates, many people felt you deserved to win, but in the end you tied for first with Carlsen, who won thanks to a rather controversial tiebreak.

'No, I was not disappointed, I was very happy...'

Come on...
'No, again, I never played for result. I was very happy after the tournament, because I knew that I played well.'

But you hoped to earn the right to play another title match against Anand.
'No, to show a good level. I understand that you may not believe this, but I was very glad after the tournament. I knew I had done very good work in my preparation, and I played well. OK, it so happened that I didn't win. If I had won on top of all this, that would have been fantastic, but it was enough for me to be happy. Everybody around me was feeling, what a pity, you played so well, but frankly I myself didn't feel like this at all.

'I remember some years ago, there was the Rapid and Blitz World Championship in Doha. Magnus

'All my inner chess education was rebelling against this wish to play like the computer.'

won the rapid and then shared first/second in the blitz. Karjakin had the better tiebreak and won, and Magnus was second. And he was completely unhappy at the closing ceremony. For me that was crazy. You played extremely well, and OK, it happened and in the blitz luck was not on your side. But he played both tournaments extremely well. That's already more than enough. For me this was beyond comprehension.'

You say, you may not believe me, but many people will find it hard to believe.
'Yes, I understand that, and they may think that I am inventing something, but I am just telling you the truth. I was perfectly fine with it.'

We shall blame your artistic background for that.
'I came to understand that with such an attitude I should not even become World Champion. Let alone three times. For me it's a kind of blessing, a present, to become World Champion when you don't want to (laughs), when actually you don't care so much (keeps laughing). Maybe it's some present for my devotion, but I honestly think that purely result-wise I achieved much more than I should have. So I have no regrets about what I didn't win. I lost the match to Vishy, we were more or less equal at that time; something went wrong. But all in all it's a miracle. If I had not become World Champion, I would have been perfectly happy. I would still believe that what I had done was fantastic. And you ask me if it's a pity I didn't play Magnus (laughs); no it's not a pity.'

When I spoke to Kasparov after he quit, he was trying to put himself in some historical perspective. He had played a match against Smyslov, worked with Botvinnik, even played Magnus. How would you see yourself from a historical perspective?
'To begin with, I am a bit different from Garry. I don't have that habit

'I found it very funny that in the end AlphaZero, learning chess by itself, discovered that the best defence against 1.e4 is the Berlin.'

to look at myself from a historical perspective. But if you force me to... I still played a couple of rapid games against Mikhail Tal and of course I met Botvinnik and we had some conversations. I played against Karpov and Kasparov. But one thing which I believe was always my strength, was that I always let the past be the past. Of course, I tried to learn lessons, but I never looked back that much. I have already travelled to another city, I am not there anymore.'

But at least we'll still have you around as AlphaZero.
'(Smiles) I have been invited to give a lecture in May at a forum in Geneva about Artificial Intelligence organized by the United Nations. Not only on AlphaZero, but also about AI. DeepMind has also been invited and they asked me as a speaker together with them, so I will dig deeper into this AlphaZero business. (Starts laughing) But of course I found it very funny that in the end AlphaZero, learning chess by itself, discovered that the best defence against 1.e4 is the Berlin.'

You weren't afraid that you were giving away the secret there?
'(Laughs) I just thought it was very funny. (Pauses) In fact, as we are talking about the end of my career, there is one thing I'd like to try to explain – something so many people have wondered about, my recurring over-optimism in my last games as a chess player. I was thinking how it got there. There were two parts. First of all, at some point, I wanted to enjoy chess, to play free chess. And secondly, it was an artificial way to revive my motivation. Like a boxer who gets tired of boxing and

suddenly wants a street fight without gloves to reignite his interest. Or, if you want, new adrenaline. I wanted new adrenaline, and I wanted a street fight. That was why I was going wild and crazy, sacrificing, risking a lot. A way to keep going. Maybe if I hadn't done this, I would probably already have stopped in 2015.

'This over-optimism has two further aspects. The first one is connected with style. If you are over-stepping the mark, you have to be optimistic, otherwise it will surely not work. The only way is to believe in your chances, even if they are only 40 per cent instead of 60.

'The second one is a deeper matter. It was a putsch, my strike against modern chess. The ideal of the modern chess player is to play according to the computer. The first line; that is the ideal. But are you really interested in following a world championship for computers? It's a fantastic level of chess, but it's just not interesting. Because there is no human touch. And all my inner chess education was rebelling against this wish to play like the computer. Chess should be something personal. If your goal is to be like a computer, it loses the main point for me: that it's a game, that it's life, a human creation. I had these discussions with seconds, yes, I know I am worse according to the computer, but I want to play like this. I know I can lose, I know I am risking too much, but I like my position and I don't care. And of course, I was not completely inadequate. I was still number 5 and even number 2 when I was playing like this. It was a little protest, but against no one. Not against other players, not against time. Whatever it was, I wanted to do it my way.' ∎

Talent Watch

Promises and prodigies in Challengers have to be patient

Magnus Carlsen observes the game between the youngest (13) and the oldest participant (52) in the Challengers (0-1, 51).

The Tata Steel Challengers is an ideal launch pad for future champions. This time, Vladislav Kovalev, at 25 already an experienced GM, finished first and earned promotion to next year's Masters. **ERWIN L'AMI** is convinced that in the coming years, several of the 'kids' will also fulfil their dreams.

Back in 2004, when my countryman Jan Smeets was preparing for the C-Group in Wijk aan Zee, he expressed his concern about a particular participant he would be facing. His name was Magnus Carlsen, a young boy from Norway, who Jan felt could be a really dangerous opponent. As I tried to reassure Jan, I explained to him that many talents had visited Wijk aan Zee before and not all of them had succeeded. I was sure this new Norwegian kid would be shown his place! As we all know now, things took quite a different turn...

The C-Group no longer exists in the Tata Steel Chess tournament, but the second group, the Challengers, remains a platform for young talents to show their strength. For this year's edition, a fine selection of young rising stars was invited – youngsters that, thanks to remarkable achievements, are rapidly becoming household names.

In this article I will take a closer look at these new 'kids', but first let me mention that first place, and promotion to next year's Masters, was claimed by Vladislav Kovalev. The 25-year-old Belarusian grandmaster won convincingly – seven wins, six draws, no losses – and it will be interesting to see how he will perform at the highest level next year.

After winning the 2018 Aeroflot Open and doing well in Dortmund last summer, Kovalev has now joined the 2700 Club. In Wijk aan Zee, his games were not spectacular, but his grinding powers were impressive! The following fragment is a good example of a vintage Kovalev win: he never shies away from a fight and grabs his chances when he gets them.

Benjamin Gledura
Vladislav Kovalev
Wijk aan Zee 2019 (5)

position after 18...♘b6

With 19.♗d2 White could have played for a small advantage but Gledura sets the board on fire with:
19.d5!? ♗xd5 Accepting the challenge! Instead, 19...♘xd5 20.exd6 (20.♕xa4 ♘c3! 21.bxc3 ♗xc3 loses

'Thanks to remarkable achievements, these youngsters are rapidly becoming household names.'

an exchange) 20...♕c8 would be more or less balanced.
20.♘d4

20...f4 Throwing more oil on the fire. Black had a few good alternatives, of which 20...♕e8 21.exd6 ♕g6 was perhaps the most straightforward one. Black is threatening ...f5-f4, as well as taking back the pawn on d6.
21.♘gf5 ♖xf5 22.♘xf5 ♕f8

This is Black's idea, and it looks very strong! But looks may deceive, as we will see shortly.
23.♘d4
23.♕c2! would have repelled the black initiative. Black could still try to fish in muddy waters with 23...f3 24.gxf3 ♗b3 25.♕e4 ♖e8, but 26.♕g4 ♔h7 27.♗f4, followed by ♔h2, ♖g1 etc, leaves little to the imagination. What follows now is a ruthless finish by Kovalev, his trademark!
23...c5 24.♘f3 24.♘b5 ♗b3! 25.♕f1 ♗c4 is an awkward pin.

24...♗b3 25.♕d3 ♗c4 26.♕c2 d5 27.e6 ♗xe2 28.♕xe2 ♘c4 29.♘e5 ♘xe5 30.♕xe5

30...♕d6! The endgame is hopeless.
31.♗xf4 ♕xe5 32.♗xe5 ♖e8 33.♖d1 ♖xe6 34.♗c3 ♗xc3 35.bxc3 c6 36.c4 dxc4!
No complexes! Accepting the triple pawns is without doubt the most convincing way to convert the endgame.

37.f3 37.♔f1 ♔f7 38.♖c1 ♖e4 is easy as well. Black will bring his king over to the c-pawns and all pawn endings are winning.
37...♖e3 38.♖c1 ♖xa3 39.♖xc4 ♖a1+ 40.♔f2 a3 41.♖xc5 a2 42.♖c2 Or 42.♖a5 c5. **42...♖f1+** White resigned.

Of course, at 25, Kovalev is still young, but even he must feel rather 'old' in the company of the new 'kids' that we will have a look at.

'Praggu glanced at the board for a second and grabbed the black queen to move it to f1!.'

I will do so by slowly moving up in the final standings. Let's begin with Rameshbabu Praggnanandhaa, the 13-year-old boy wonder from India. Praggnanandhaa has been making headlines for some time already, initially for becoming the youngest International Master in history at the age of 10 years and 10 months, and after that for trying to beat Sergey Karjakin's record of youngest grandmaster in history. In the end, 'Praggu' needed 3 months more than Sergey, becoming a GM at the age of 12 years and 10 months.

Praggu sees tactics lightning-fast, which I noticed first-hand when I was analysing my game against Lucas van Foreest. I had escaped with a draw and the post-mortem showed many attractive continuations for my opponent. At some point, we were looking at this position:

I was just about to agree that the position was bad for me (I was Black), when Praggu passed by, glanced at the board for a second and grabbed the black queen to move it to f1!
Of course, being as young as he is, Praggu's play has not yet matured, which led to some incomprehensible moments.

Rameshbabu Praggnanandhaa
Maksim Chigaev
Wijk aan Zee 2019 (10)

position after 39.♖a5

White had missed a direct win in the middlegame and instead reached a pawn-up endgame in which Praggu went astray. In the diagrammed position, Black is already comfortable. He can draw with 39...f3+ 40.♔xf3 ♖d3+ 41.♔e2 ♖d2+, when 42.♔e1 ♔e4 is a dangerous winning attempt for White, so he is best advised to repeat with 42.♔f3. Chigaev, however, found a better try:
39...♖d2+!? 40.♔xd2 fxg3+

41.♔d3!
Not 41.♔e2 gxh2 42.♖xe5+ ♔f6!, when the white king prevents the rook from getting to e1, or 41.♔d1 gxh2 42.♖xe5+ ♔xe5 43.♗g3+, when Black does not play 43...♗f4, but goes 43...♔e4 44.♗xh2 ♔f3 and promotes his h-pawn after ...♔g2 and ...♗h4-g3.
41...gxh2 42.♖xe5+ ♔xe5 43.♗g3+ ♗f4 44.♗xh2 ♗xh2
With the dust cleared, Black remains saddled with the infamous 'wrong bishop', so all that remains for White

is to bring the king to h1. Praggu spent five seconds on:

45.♔e3??
Needless to say, 45.♔e2 ♔f4 46.♔f2 ♔g4 47.a4 is a draw. Black will have to move the bishop from h2 to stop the queenside pawns, after which the white king will be tucked away on h1.
45...♗g3! 46.♔f3 ♗e1

Now the white king can't move and it's up to the black king to round up the queenside pawns. That's an easy job.
47.a4 ♔d5 48.a5 ♔c5 49.b3 ♔b5 50.b4 ♗h4 51.c4+ ♔a6

White resigned. After 52.c5 ♔b5 he is in zugzwang and will lose all his pawns.

Heart-breaking. With a final score of -3 this was clearly not Praggnanandhaa's tournament, but he is so young that it's hard to draw any conclusions from this result. I simply think that playing a 13-round event of this calibre was a great experience for the young Indian. With the experienced coach Ramesh by his side, they will surely draw the right conclusions before moving on to new heights.

Germany's big hope

Vincent Keymer shocked the chess world by winning the strong 2018 Grenke Open. With this sensational victory, the 13-year-old (at the time; he was born November 15, 2004) qualified for this year's main event which will feature the world elite, including Magnus Carlsen. Vincent is working with Peter Leko and already has a very serious opening repertoire. 1.d4 is met by the Semi-Tarrasch, while 1.e4 is met with the Najdorf. I have played Keymer on two occasions and got good to winning positions in both games. Still, both of them ended in a draw and what remained was the feeling that I had played someone very resourceful and tenacious. Those are good characteristics!

Erwin l'Ami
Vincent Keymer
Wijk aan Zee 2019 (11)

position after 44...♗e7

I should probably reroute my knight to d3 before starting any queenside operations, but I did not see what was wrong with: **45.b5**

Vincent Keymer (14) has the right characteristics to become a top player and he has the right coach, former World Championship finalist Peter Leko.

Vincent immediately punished my hasty decision with **45...♖f8 46.♘f2 axb5! 47.cxb5 ♖a8!**
This whole operation came as a total surprise to me. Was I just going to get a free passed pawn?
48.♖a1 ♔d7 49.♘d3 hxg3 50.hxg3 ♗d8! 51.a6 bxa6 52.bxa6 ♗b6!

And here everything became clear. My a-pawn is no powerhouse and Black's bishop is a monster on b6. The game was soon drawn (½-½, 64).

Perhaps not an overly exciting example, but I think many players would have defended passively and ended up in trouble.

The following example shows Keymer's eye for the king.

Vincent Keymer
Dinara Saduakassova
Wijk aan Zee 2019 (8)

position after 31...♕a6

Vincent continues in an instructive manner:
32.♖xc4! dxc4
Black needs to keep the b-file closed, as 32...bxc4 33.♖a1 ♕b6 34.♖b1 ♕c7 35.♕f3 causes an immediate collapse. Black can't protect both f5 and the b8-square. Note that 35...♕xe5 36.♘c6 ♕f6 37.♗e3! is of no help either.
33.♕f3!

33...♛b6

33...♝d7! keeps Black in the game, as the endgames after both 34.♝xf8 ♝xf8 35.♛d5 ♝e6 36.♛xb5 ♛xb5 37.♘xb5 and 34.e6 fxe6 35.♛g3 ♘g6 36.♛b8+ ♚c8 37.♛xc8+ ♝xc8 are tenable.

34.♘c6

The point. A very important defender of the black king is eliminated.

34...♝c5 35.♛g3 ♘g6 36.♛g5 ♝f8 37.♝xf8 ♚g8

Because 37...♘xf8 runs into 38.♛f6+ ♚g8 39.♘e7 mate.

38.♝h6

Black resigned. Mate is imminent.

The upcoming Grenke Classic will be a great challenge for Keymer. Quite frankly, I believe the tournament comes a bit too early in his career. But then I have been proven wrong before!

Steady progress

Lucas van Foreest (17) comes from a big chess family, of which his brother Jorden, his sister Machteld, and Lucas himself are the most famous exponents. Lucas (born March 3, 2001) is making steady progress and left a good impression in Wijk aan Zee. Following the Dutch school of Euwe and Timman, Lucas is very much up to date on the latest opening news and is already a pretty all-round player. While there are still big steps to be made, he can occasionally already do things like this:

Lucas van Foreest
Evgeny Bareev
Wijk aan Zee 2019 (3)

position after 21...♜c6

Structurally speaking, Black is in charge, but it's all about the king here!

22.♛h4 ♚f8 23.♛h8+ ♘g8 24.♜h7 f6 Black seems to have set up a good line of defence, and it's not immediately evident how White can increase the pressure.

25.♘f3 ♜xc3 26.♘e5!

This had to have been seen on move 22, as otherwise White's attack hits a dead end.

26...fxe5 27.fxe5 Inviting the a1-rook to the party! **27...♜f3** The only move, but at a high cost! **28.gxf3 ♜b8 29.f4** 29.♚h1 would probably have been better, preventing the defence Black could have tried in the game. **29...♛c7 30.f5 exf5** 30...gxf5 31.♚h1!, followed by ♜g1, was the other point behind 30.f5 ! **31.♜e1 ♜b7**

31...♜b2!, with the idea of 32.e6 ♜e2!!, was an amazing defence! Now 33.♜xe2 ♛c1+ is perpetual check.

32.♖h3! ♛a5 33.♖h4 ♘e7

33...g5 34.♛f2 g6 was tougher, but should also lose in the long run.

34.e6 ♛d2 35.♖b3!

Black resigned in view of the line 35...♖xb3 36.♛h8+ ♘g8 37.e7+, when White promotes with check.

On the brink of 2700

World Junior Champion Parham Maghsoodloo (born August 12, 2000) must have found his first visit to the Dutch coast rather disappointing. Going in as one of the favourites, Parham never managed to be in contention for first place. After a first-round loss to Anton Korobov the Iranian did strike back in the next two rounds, but a loss against Chigaev in Round 8 put an end to any dreams of promoting to the 2020 Masters. Parham did occasionally show what he is capable of, and at 18 he is on the brink of 2700. I am sure we will hear much more from him.

His win against Evgeny Bareev, winner in Wijk aan Zee in 2002, was perhaps his most creative achievement. (Seeing Bareev lose two games within a couple of pages, you may get a distorted imagine of his tournament. In fact, the former Candidate scored a respectable 7 out of 13!)

Parham Maghsoodloo
Evgeny Bareev
Wijk aan Zee 2019 (10)
Caro-Kann, Advance Variation

1.e4 c6

Bareev's lifelong opening, the Caro-Kann. Maghsoodloo treats it in the sharpest way imaginable.

2.d4 d5 3.e5 ♗f5 4.♘c3 e6 5.g4 ♗g6 6.♘ge2 c5 7.h4 h5 8.♘f4 ♗h7

9.g5!?

A relatively fresh attempt at an opening advantage. The old move 9.♘xh5 is no longer considered to be very dangerous. For more details, I would obviously refer you to the DVD of Vidit Gujrathi.

9...♘c6

9...cxd4 10.♘b5 ♗e4 11.f3 ♗f5 12.♘xd4 ♘e7 is a reliable way for Black to play. The game continuation is an attempt to refute White's 9th move.

10.♛xh5 ♘xd4

11.♘xe6

11.♗e3 ♘xc2+ 12.♔d2 is fine for Black, as long as he doesn't play 12...♘xa1 13.♗b5+ ♔e7 14.♗xc5+. Instead, 12...♘e7 13.♗xe6 ♛b6 14.♗b5+ ♘c6 15.♘xd5 ♖d8! leads to interesting complications. Another pretty line is 12...♘d4 13.♗xd4 cxd4 14.♗b5+ ♔e7 15.g6 dxc3+ 16.bxc3 ♗xg6 17.♛xg6 fxg6 18.♘xg6+ ♔f7 19.♘xh8+ ♔e7 20.♘g6+, with perpetual check.

11...♘xe6 12.♗b5+ ♔e7

Parham Maghsoodloo (18) only showed flashes of his undeniable potential.

13.g6

Parham was still very much blitzing his moves, but here there was an interesting alternative in 13.♗e3!?, after which 13...a6 14.0-0-0 axb5 15.♘xd5+ ♔e8 16.♘f6+ gxf6 17.♖xd8+ ♖xd8 (17...♘xd8!?) 18.exf6 leads to a pretty irrational position. It's hard to judge the consequences of 18...♘xf6 19.gxf6 ♗e4 20.♛xh8 ♗xh1, but the computer seems to think there is some dynamic equality. Black can also go all out with 13...♘xc2!? 14.♛xh8 d4. Homework for you, dear reader ☺.

13...♗xg6

13...fxg6 14.♛f3 leads to mate.

14.♛xh8 d4 15.♗g5+ ♘xg5

16.hxg5 Even more dangerous looks 16.0-0-0!?, when Black faces a tough choice. Probably best is 16...♘e4 17.♘xe4 ♗xe4 18.♖he1 ♘h6 19.♖xe4 ♕d5 20.♕h7 ♕xa2 21.c3 ♕b3 (not 21...dxc3 22.♖d7+ ♔e6 23.♗c4+!) 22.e6 ♕xb5 (22...f5 23.♖ee1 ♕xb5 24.♕g6 followed by ♕g5 and e7, is crushing) 23.exf7+ ♔d7 24.♖de1 dxc3 25.bxc3 ♕a6!! 26.♖e8 g6!! 27.♖xa8 ♕a1+, with a perpetual. Good luck finding that sequence over the board!

16...dxc3 17.♖d1

17...♕c7

If Black wants to sacrifice his queen, he should do so with 17...cxb2 18.0-0 (18.♖xd8 b1♕+!) 18...♕c7 19.♖d7+ ♕xd7 20.♗xd7 ♔xd7, with enough compensation, as we are about to see. The game continuation allows White an improvement over this variation. In the pressroom, Parham showed the line 17...♕a5 18.♖d7+ ♔e6 19.♕h3+ ♗f5 20.♖d6+ ♔xd6 21.♗c4+ ♔e7 22.♕xf5 cxb2+ 23.♔e2 ♖e8 24.♖d1 ♕a4 25.♗xf7 ♗c7 26.c4, which, as you can imagine, led to lively analysis! The conclusion was that Black should hold.

18.♖d7+

18.bxc3!, eliminating the strong and potentially passed pawn, was the way forward! White is now ready to go ♖d7+, while the knight on g8 is still hanging as well. Black can't survive.

18...♕xd7 19.♗xd7 cxb2!
19...♔xd7 20.♕h3+! would make Black lose his biggest asset.

20.0-0 ♔xd7 21.♕xg8

A curious position. I believed that with two bishops and that huge pawn on b2, Black should have plenty of compensation for the queen. He has to be a bit careful, though.

21...c4 22.♕h8

White's queen rushes back. 22.e6+!? works well after 22...♔xe6 23.♕h8!, when the black king is out in the open, but 22...fxe6 23.♖d1+ ♔e7 24.♖e1 ♗e4! 25.g6 ♔d6 is still very messy and unclear.

22...♔c7

Black caves in under the pressure. The only move was 22...♗xc2 23.♕h3+ ♔c6!, and now 24.♕c3 b1♕ 25.♖xb1 ♗xb1 26.♕xc4+ ♗c5 27.♕a4+ b5 28.♕a6+ ♗b6 29.a4 ♗d3 30.a5 ♖d8 31.axb6 axb6 is very drawish. It is likely that 23.♕h1!? was what bothered Bareev, but here Black

escapes with 23...♔c7 24.♕d5 ♖c8!?, with the idea of 25.♕xc4+ ♔b8 26.♕b5 ♗a3!, and the pawn remains very much alive.

23.♕h4 ♖c8

24.♕d4! Taking the b-pawn off the board changes the picture.
24...♗xc2 25.♕xb2 ♗f5 26.g6 fxg6 27.e6 ♖e8 28.♕b5 ♖xe6 29.♕xc4+ ♔b8 30.♖d1 ♖e8 31.♕f4+ Black resigned. He will indeed lose more material after 31...♔a8 32.♕c7 a6 33.♖d8+.

The real deal from Russia
From all the youngsters that played in the Challengers, 16-year-old Andrey Esipenko is perhaps least known to the general public, but the gifted Russian is the real deal! To remind you, at the 2017 Rapid World Championship in Riyadh, he played what was perhaps the most beautiful move of the tournament – against none other than Sergey Karjakin.

Karjakin-Esipenko
Riyadh rapid 2017
position after 22.♔a1

22...♕b3!!
Need I say more? ☺

Andrey had a great tournament in Wijk aan Zee, and going into the last round he was still in the running for promotion to the Masters. Unfortunately for him, he suffered his only loss that day (against Evgeny Bareev!) and finished in shared second place, one and a half points behind Vladislav Kovalev.

Esipenko has a remarkably good feel for the game for his age, and he will no doubt enter the world's top 100 soon. I can't imagine that his ambitions will end there, though! Andrey was kind enough to analyse his game versus Korobov, in which he resurrected the famous ♘xf7 sacrifice that Topalov famously introduced against Kramnik in Wijk aan Zee in 2008.

NOTES BY
Andrey Esipenko

Andrey Esipenko
Anton Korobov
Wijk aan Zee 2019 (7)
Semi-Slav

1.d4 d5 2.c4 c6 3.♘f3 ♘f6 4.♘c3 e6

I knew that Anton Korobov mainly leans towards the Slav, although he has a broad opening repertoire.

5.♗g5 h6 6.♗h4 dxc4 7.e4 g5 8.♗g3 b5 9.♗e2

The Anti-Moscow Variation. Here Black has several good continuations, but Anton follows the main line.

9...♗b7
Now White has a wide choice of

moves, but the knight sacrifice on move 12 very much appealed to me and I decided to try it.

10.♘e5 ♘bd7 11.0-0 ♗g7
The main move. After 11...h5 12.♘xd7 ♕xd7 13.♕c1 ♖g8 14.♖d1, White's position looks highly promising.

12.♘xf7!?
I directly witnessed the game Grischuk-Ding Liren from the 2018 Candidates Tournament in Berlin, and already then I decided that from the practical point of view it was a very interesting continuation. After looking at it a little before the game, I saw my feeling confirmed, although nevertheless there were certain fears. 12.♘xd7 is mainly played, but I did not like the fact that my opponent would be prepared for this line.

12...♔xf7 13.e5

13...♘d5
There is also another line: 13...♘e8 (defending the d6-point) 14.♗h5+ ♔g8 15.f4 ♖h7. The only move, as otherwise Black stands badly. 16.f5 exf5 17.♖xf5 c5 18.d5 ♘xe5 19.♗xe5 ♗xe5 20.♖xe5 ♗e7 21.♖e6 ♖xe6 22.dxe6 ♕d4+ 23.♕xd4 cxd4

24.♘xb5 ♘f6 25.♗f7+ ♔f8 26.♘xd4 ♗e4 and Black is close to equality. Of course, with correct play Black can make a draw in all variations, but often 'inconceivable' moves have to be made.

14.♘e4 ♕b6 15.♘d6+ ♔e7

The key position.
16.a4!?
This seems to be the most dangerous move for Black. 16.♗g4 has mainly been played, but this is an inaccuracy: 16...h5! 17.♗xh5 ♖af8 18.♕g4 ♗h6 19.b4 and this is much simpler for Black to play than White. (After the logical 19.h4 c5 20.hxg5 ♗g7, White's position is hopeless. This variation shows how delicate this position is, and how after essentially making one logical but inaccurate move, it is possible to lose immediately.) For instance, 16.♕c2?! ♕xd4 17.♖ad1 ♕b6 18.♖fe1 ♗xe5 19.♗g4 ♗xg3 20.♖xe6+ ♔d8 21.hxg3 ♘c7 22.b3 cxb3 and Black has repulsed the attack and White is still a piece down.

16...a5?
I think that my opponent wanted to immediately dislodge me from

Is Andrey Esipenko (16) the great promise Russia has been waiting for? After his second place in the Challengers he looks ready for more.

my preparation, because this does not look a logical move. But I had not done much preparation in this line. I had only outlined the plans, thinking that with such a knight I would always have good play, whereas for Black it was possibly more difficult from the practical point of view to play this position.
The Grischuk-Ding Liren game went 16...♖af8! (the best move) 17.♗f3 a6 (the most logical) 18.♗xd5. This is White's idea – to first exchange Black's strong knight, and then prepare and carry out f2-f4. 18...cxd5 19.axb5 axb5 20.♔h1

ANALYSIS DIAGRAM

In my preparations this position appealed to me for White. Of course,

for the computer everything here is a draw, but for a human it is a very complicated problem. If even Ding Liren played this position inaccurately (the game ended in a draw, but at one point he erred and could have lost), it shows how difficult this position is to play with Black.

17.♗f3

Possibly a slight inaccuracy. 17.♗g4!? was stronger, but I could not work out the advantages of this variation compared with 16.♗g4 h5. 17...h5 18.♗xh5 ♖af8 19.♕g4 ♗h6 20.♖fd1 and then h2-h4, with the initiative. During the game I could not altogether understand what was happening, so I simply decided to carry out Grischuk's plan (♗xd5, ♔h1 and f2-f4).

17...♖hf8?

The decisive mistake; my opponent obviously lost the thread of the game. In the computer's opinion, much stronger was 17...bxa4 and now I would definitely not have played 18.♗g4, because it is not logical to lose a tempo for no apparent reason, even if the computer suggests this. But I would have played 18.♕c2 ♕xd4 19.♖fd1 ♕a7 20.♘xc4, with a very complicated position.

18.♗xd5 cxd5 19.axb5

Now, when White advances f2-f4, Black's position will collapse.

19...♖f5

The best chance, I think.

20.♔h1

Of course, there is no need to take the rook, since in this position the knight is much stronger than the rook.

20...♔f8 21.f4 ♔g8

22.♘xf5

Now is the time to exchange, because I also pick up several pawns and in addition my rook and queen begin attacking the opponent's king.

22...exf5 23.fxg5 ♘f8

Trying to occupy strong squares, but this does not work.

**24.gxh6 ♕xh6 25.♖xf5 ♗c8
26.♖f1 ♗e6**

White's position seems completely winning, but I sensed that I was beginning to lose the thread of the play. I nevertheless endeavoured to compose myself and see the game through to a win.

27.♕e1 ♕g6

28.♕d2

Not a logical move, and I myself did not really understand the point of it. Most probably I simply wanted to consolidate the position and placed the queen on a more active square. Here I considered 28.♗h4 ♗f5, when I was intending 29.♖a3, but then I noticed 29...♗d3 and I realized that all was not so simple. Instead of ♖a3 the computer suggests very many winning moves, but they are not very logical.

28...♘d7

Here my opponent was already in time-trouble, whereas I had sufficient time to calculate the variations.

29.♗h4 ♗h6

Now 29...♗f5 is worse than in the earlier variation, because the black knight has already moved to d7 and

is out of play. On e6 it would have put more pressure on White's position. After 30.♖xa5 White wins.

30.♕e1

The knight on d7 is covering the f6-square, but it cannot come into play.

30...♕e4 31.♕f2 ♔h7

More resilient was 31...♕e3 32.♕xe3 ♗xe3 33.♗f2, but White has too many pawns.

32.♖a3 ♖f8 33.♗f6 ♘xf6 34.exf6 ♗g5 35.b6 ♖xf6 36.♖f3

Black cannot cope with the pawn on b6.

36...♖xf3 37.♕xf3 ♕xd4 38.♕g3 ♗f6 39.b7 ♗e5 40.b8♕ ♗xg3 41.hxg3 Black resigned.

Rounding off, it is tempting to ask the question of how many of these youngsters we will be seeing in the Tata Steel Masters in the coming years? My prediction is at least three!

Addendum

After filing my report, the editor-in-chief of this magazine felt that 'a certain game' from the last round was missing. Needless to say, I had no problems correcting that error!

NOTES BY
Erwin l'Ami

**Erwin l'Ami
Elisabeth Paehtz**
Wijk aan Zee 2019 (13)
Queen's Pawn Opening

1.d4 e6 2.c4 ♗b4+ 3.♗d2 a5

Certainly not what I had expected for this game, hence my modest reply.

4.e3 b6

Perhaps 4...♘f6, preventing my next move, was more natural, though it's not at all clear whether it should be stopped at all.

5.♕g4

Going for a type of Bogo-Indian/Winawer position; not your most common hybrid!

5...♗f6

5...♘f6 6.♕xg7 ♖g8 7.♕h6 does not provide much compensation, but 5...g6 should be entirely playable. Black will follow up with ...♗b7 and ...f5.

6.♘c3 ♗b7

7.♘f3

Both 7.f3, making the bishop on b7 unhappy, and 7.a3, forcing Black to take on c3, were better options.

Multi-talented. While Erwin l'Ami combined playing in the Challengers with being our reporter, his wife Alina combined being one of the official tournament photographers with sitting on the armrest of his chair!

14...♘e7

14...d5 15.cxd5 ♗xd5 16.♘d2 ♘b4 looks annoying, but 17.e4! changes everything. Now 17...♘c2+ 18.♔d1 ♘xa1 19.exd5 is just lost, since the a1-knight will be picked up later, and 17...♘c6 18.♔d1 is also nicer for White.

15.d5

15...♔f7 I considered 15...e5 16.a4 ♘c5 17.♘d2 to be lost for Black. I'll go b3 and ♔d1-c2 and prepare to open the kingside with f2-f4. Black is essentially a piece down with the bishop on b7.

16.♘d4 exd5 17.♘b5

Starting with 17.♖d1 would have been preferable, but I had underestimated Black's defence on move 17.

17...♔e6

I thought that 17...♗c6! 18.♘xd6+ ♔e6 19.♘b5 ♗xb5 20.cxb5 ♘c5 was

7...h5 8.♕g3 ♗d6 9.♕g5 ♕xg5
10.♘xg5 f6 I had expected 10...♗e7, when 11.h4 promises White a small but pleasant endgame advantage due to his extra space.
11.♘f3 g5 12.♘b5!
Going after the bishop pair.
12...♘a6 13.♘xd6+ cxd6 14.♗c3
Preparing the d4-d5 break. The less creative 14.♗e2 was not bad either, preparing 0-0, ♖fc1, ♘e1 and f3.

better for White. In reality, however, her knights have great outposts, while the king also does a good job on e6. Black is probably perfectly alright.

18.♖d1

Threatening e3-e4!.

18...♘f5 19.cxd5+ ♗xd5 20.♖xd5

I have many attractive options here, of which 20.♗xf6 is perhaps the easiest. But I could not resist the game continuation.

20...♔xd5 21.e4+

Luring the king in even deeper.

21...♔xe4 22.♗c4!

Important! Now that the king has left d5, the door is immediately shut.

22...d5 23.f3+ ♔f4

24.♗xd5

Truth be told, I had planned 24.♔f2 when playing 20.♖xd5. At this point, though, I realized that 24...dxc4 would be a pretty cold shower, since Black can always give up her f5-knight and then use that square to tuck away the king.

24.♗d3 ♘b4 25.♗b1 d4! did not look clear either, so by elimination I arrived at the game continuation.

24...g4 After the game Elisabeth proposed 24...♖ac8 as a better defence, which is certainly correct. I would have had to go 25.g3+ ♘xg3 26.hxg3+ ♔xg3 27.♘d6, when there is still a struggle ahead.

25.0-0

A pleasant move to make. ☺

25...♘e3 25...g3 26.♗d2+ ♔e5 27.♗f7! would have made for a pretty finish. There is no stopping ♖e1+ without losing a lot of material.

25...♔g5 26.fxg4 hxg4 27.♗d2+ ♔g6 28.♗e4 is no solution either.

26.g3+ ♔f5 Or 26...♔g5 27.♗d2!, winning the knight.

27.fxg4+ ♔g6 28.♖xf6+ ♔g5

29.♗xa8 Materialistic! 29.♘d6 ♔xg4 (29...♘xd5 30.♘e4+ ♔xg4 31.♘f2+ ♔g5 32.h4 mate) 30.♗f3+ ♔h3 31.♘e4 and mate on the next move was the proper way to end it!

29...♖xa8 30.♘d6 ♔xg4 31.♗d2 ♘d5 32.♔g2!

Black resigned. There is not stopping h2-h3, mate. ■

Wijk aan Zee 2019 – Challengers cat. XIV

					1	2	3	4	5	6	7	8	9	10	11	12	13	14		TPR
1	Vladislav Kovalev	IGM	BLR	2687	*	½	1	½	½	½	½	1	1	1	½	1	1	1	10	2782
2	Andrey Esipenko	IGM	RUS	2584	½	*	½	½	1	½	0	½	1	1	1	1	½	½	8½	2689
3	Benjamin Gledura	IGM	HUN	2615	0	½	*	1	½	1	½	½	½	1	1	½	1	½	8½	2687
4	Maksim Chigaev	IGM	RUS	2604	½	½	0	*	½	½	½	1	½	½	1	1	1	1	8½	2688
5	Anton Korobov	IGM	UKR	2699	½	0	½	½	*	½	½	1	½	1	½	½	½	1	7½	2627
6	Erwin l'Ami	IGM	NED	2643	½	½	0	½	½	*	1	½	½	½	½	½	1	1	7½	2632
7	Evgeny Bareev	IGM	CAN	2650	½	1	½	½	½	0	*	0	0	½	1	1	½	1	7	2603
8	Parham Maghsoodloo	IGM	IRI	2679	0	½	½	0	0	½	1	*	½	½	½	1	1	1	7	2601
9	Lucas van Foreest	IGM	NED	2502	0	0	½	½	½	½	1	½	*	½	½	½	1	0	6	2557
10	Vincent Keymer	IM	GER	2500	0	0	0	½	0	½	½	½	½	*	½	1	½	1	5½	2529
11	Rameshbabu Praggnanandhaa	IGM	IND	2539	½	0	0	0	½	½	0	½	½	½	*	½	½	1	5	2496
12	Dinara Saduakassova	IM	KAZ	2472	0	0	½	0	½	½	0	0	½	0	½	*	½	½	3½	2413
13	Elisabeth Paehtz	IM	GER	2477	0	½	0	0	½	0	½	0	0	½	½	½	*	½	3½	2413
14	Stefan Kuipers	IM	NED	2470	0	½	½	0	0	0	0	0	1	0	0	½	½	*	3	2377

SECRETS OF OPENING SURPRISES

Surprises by the Dutch seaside

Jeroen Bosch

The 81st edition of the Tata Steel Chess Tournament had an almost ideal line-up: the World Champion, several elite players and a fine choice of ambitious GMs hoping to make an impression. Such a mix often produces great fighting chess, and, since this is Wijk aan Zee, a familiar winner. From our SOS perspective, the harvest was definitely rich.

Vladimir Kramnik
Anish Giri
Wijk aan Zee 2019 (2)
English Opening, Four Knights System

1.c4 e5 2.♘c3 ♘f6 3.♘f3 ♘c6
In my previous column (2019/1), I mentioned several less theoretical options for White on move four in the English Four Knights. One of these options was: **4.d3!?**

Giri now went for one of the critical responses with **4...d5!? 5.cxd5 ♘xd5** when Kramnik decided to go for the 'Sveshnikov' move **6.e4!? ♘xc3**
Giri opts for quick development, but improves White's structure. There is nothing very wrong with taking, but the resulting position is harder to play for Black. He will have to take measures against both d3-d4 and f2-f4, while lacking an active plan.
7.bxc3 ♗c5 To prevent a future d3-d4, Black places his bishop on the a7-g1 diagonal.

8.♗e2 0-0 9.0-0 ♗b6
9...♔h8 10.♖b1 ♖b8 11.♘xe5!? ♘xe5 12.d4 ♗d6 13.dxe5 ♗xe5, and now, rather than the time-consuming 14.♕a4 ♗d7 15.♕xa7 b6!, Tal-Chernin, Sochi 1986, White should have played 14.♗e3, when White has still some chances for an opening edge due to his mobile pawn centre.
10.a4 ♖e8 11.♕c2
A previous game saw 11.♖b1 h6 12.♕c2 a6?! 13.♗e3 ♗xe3 14.fxe3, and White is better, since after some preparation Black will find it hard to handle d3-d4 (Svenn-Aström, Sweden 2000). However, Black should not have touched his a-pawn.
11...♕f6 12.♔h1 h6 And now after **13.♘g1** (preparing f2-f4) Kramnik had a pleasant edge.

Shankland also played an early d3 in the English Opening.

Sam Shankland
Jorden van Foreest
Wijk aan Zee 2019 (7)
English Opening

1.c4 e5 2.d3!? ♘f6 3.♘f3 ♘c6 4.a3!? As usual, White has a lot of leeway, especially in a 'slow' opening like the English.
4...d5 5.cxd5 ♘xd5
The Najdorf with colours reversed! Grischuk and Caruana played it in a couple of blitz games. The Najdorf is one of the best openings around,

and yet with a tempo up it does not necessarily yield an advantage.

6.e3

6.e4 ♘b6 7.♗e3 ♗e7 8.♘bd2 0-0 9.♖c1 ♘f6!? (preventing a possible exchange sacrifice on c6) 10.b4 a6 11.♗e2 ♖e8 12.0-0, with equal play, Grischuk-Caruana, St. Louis 2017.

6...a5 7.♗e2 ♗d6

A typical Scheveningen position arose after 7...♗e7 8.0-0 0-0 9.♕c2 ♗e6 10.b3 f5 11.♗b2 ♗f6 12.♘bd2 ♕e7 13.♖ac1 ♔h8 14.♖fe1 ♖ad8 15.♗f1 ♘b6 16.♕b1 ♗g8 17.e4 f4 18.♕c2 (18.d4!) 18...g5 19.h3 h5 20.♕c5? (20.d4) 20...♕g7, and now 21...g4 is going to be very powerful; Grischuk-Caruana, St. Louis 2017.

8.b3 0-0 9.♗b2 f5 10.♘bd2 ♕e7 11.♕c2 ♗d7 12.g3 ♔h8 13.0-0 ♖ae8

with a typically complicated Sicilian (with colours reversed) in which the chances are dynamically balanced.

In this way, Shankland decided to avoid the main lines against a young and well-prepared opponent with his 2.d3 in the English Opening. In the previous round, Jorden van Foreest had, in fact, adopted an old SOS idea versus the Pirc.

Jorden van Foreest
Vladimir Fedoseev
Wijk aan Zee 2019 (6)
Pirc Defence, Austrian Attack

1.e4 d6 2.d4 ♘f6 3.♘c3 g6 4.f4 ♗g7 5.a3!?

A golden oldie! I wrote a SOS column on this surprising move for NIC 2002/5. The idea is to prevent ...c7-c5.

5...♘c6 However, it later turned out that by sacrificing a pawn Black could execute ...c5 after all: 5...0-0 6.♘f3 c5 7.dxc5 ♕a5 8.b4 ♕c7, and Black has sufficient compensation.

6.♘f3 0-0 7.♗e2 d5

Very provocative! White has a little something after 7...♗g4 8.d5 ♘b8 9.h3 ♗xf3 10.♗xf3 c6 11.♗e3 ♘bd7 12.0-0, Anand-Nepomniachtchi, St. Louis 2017.

8.e5 ♘e4 9.♗d3 f5!? 10.0-0

Good alternatives are 10.h4 and 10.♘e2.

10...e6 11.♗e3 b6 12.♘g5? ♘xg5 13.fxg5

and now **13...f4 14.♖xf4 ♖xf4 15.♗xf4 ♘xd4 16.♗xg6 hxg6 17.♕xd4** led to unclear play, with the advantage swinging back and forth until Jorden found a lovely 39th move and won. Instead, 13...♘xe5! 14.dxe5 d4 would have saddled White with the job of re-establishing some kind of equilibrium.

Fedoseev confronted the World Champion with another old SOS idea, and the young Russian was the only player who managed to land the tournament winner in real trouble.

Vladimir Fedoseev
Magnus Carlsen
Wijk aan Zee 2019 (7)
Grünfeld Defence, Three Knights Variation

1.d4 ♘f6 2.c4 g6 3.♘c3 d5 4.♘f3

I covered 4.h4 in NIC 2004/2, but it's more accurate to play this idea by interpolating 4.♘f3 ♗g7. Black has 4...c5! after the immediate launch of the rook pawn.

4...♗g7 5.h4

5...c6 The most popular and most solid reply.

White has been doing great in the endgame after 5...c5 6.dxc5 ♕a5 7.cxd5 ♘xd5 8.♕xd5 ♗xc3+ 9.♗d2 ♗xd2+ (9...♗e6) 10.♕xd2 ♕xd2+ 11.♘xd2, Fridman-Kantans, Riga rapid 2014 (and many other games).

This line is known from the 5.♗f4 line – White has an extra (useful) tempo here: h2-h4!.

On move six, Black should investigate 6.0-0!? 7.cxd5 ♘a6 8.h5 ♘xc5 9.hxg6 fxg6 10.♗h6 ♗xh6 11.♖xh6 ♕b6 12.♖h4 ♗f5 (12...♕xb2! 13.♕c1 ♕xc1+ 14.♖xc1 is equal) 13.♕d2 ♘ce4 14.♘xe4 ♗xe4 15.d6 ♕xd6 16.♕xd6 exd6, and Black won in Inarkiev-Wei Yi, Magas 2018, but

17.♘d4! is a tiny edge for White.
6.cxd5 cxd5 7.♗f4 ♘c6 8.e3 0-0 9.♕b3 ♘a5 Some two dozen games had reached this position.
10.♕a3 The alternative is 10.♕b4 ♘c6 11.♕a3 ♗f5.
10...♘c4 10...♗f5 11.♗e2 ♘e4 12.♘xe4 ♗xe4 13.0-0 ♘c4 14.♕c3 ♖c8 was a clean equalizer in Al Sayed-Sarana, St. Petersburg 2018.

11.♗xc4 A new move. White won both games with 11.♕b4 ♕b6 12.♕xb6, but this had nothing to do with the current position.
11...dxc4 12.0-0 ♗d7 12...a6, 12...♗e6. **13.♘e5 b5 14.♕a6 ♕c8 15.♕a5 ♕d8 16.♕xd8 ♖fxd8 17.♘xd7 ♘xd7 18.♘xb5 e5 19.dxe5 ♘xe5 20.♖ac1 a6 21.♘a3 ♘d3 22.♖c2** and the extra pawn means that White can torture Black for quite a while. Carlsen had to defend an unpleasant rook ending, but managed of course! (See Jan Timman's column – ed.)

He did not repeat the Grünfeld in Wijk aan Zee, though, and went for a Queen's Gambit with an early twist in his next Black game.

Sam Shankland
Magnus Carlsen
Wijk aan Zee 2019 (9)
Queen's Gambit Declined,
Janowski Variation

1.d4 d5 2.c4 e6 3.♘c3 a6!?
The Janowski Variation of the Queen's Gambit. Alekhine and Euwe were World Champions who also adopted the little rook pawn move, and Carlsen had also played it before.

In recent times, 3...a6 has been quite popular in high-level games. It's funny: we used to tell kids that one or two pawn moves in the opening (in the centre!) were enough, and that pieces should be developed as quickly as possible, but look what the World Champion is doing in his first five moves!

The point of 3...a6 is that it more or less forces White to take on d5 – as Black might otherwise take on c4 and obtain a decent Queen's Gambit Accepted.

4.cxd5 exd5 5.♘f3
5.♗f4 ♘f6 6.e3 ♗d6 shows another point of 3...a6. Just as in the move order with 3...♗e7, White cannot develop the bishop to g5, but in addition Black can now offer the bishop swap without losing a tempo (...a6 is moderately useful).
5...h6!? Carlsen goes his own way with another waiting move.
5...c6 6.♗f4 (instead, 6.e4 dxe4 7.♘g5 was the blitz game Aronian-Carlsen, Stavanger 2016) 6...♗d6 is how this line used to be played. Euwe won all his four games as Black from this position.
Lately, however, 5...♘f6 6.♗g5 ♗e6 7.e3 ♘bd7 has been all the rage.
6.♗f4 ♘f6 7.e3
In the World Rapid Championship Carlsen had encountered 7.♕b3 ♗d6 8.♗xd6 ♕xd6 9.e3 0-0 10.♗d3 b6 11.0-0 ♘bd7 12.♖fd1 ♗b7 13.♖ac1 ♖fd8 14.♕c2 c5, Melkumyan-Carlsen, St. Petersburg 2018.
7...♗d6! and that's the point of Black's set-up. However, I guess that both players were satisfied at this

stage. It's not the type of position in which the World Champion can suddenly work miracles. **8.♗xd6 ♕xd6 9.♕c2 0-0 10.♗d3 ♖e8 11.h3 ♗e6 12.0-0 ♘bd7 13.a4?!** 13.♖ac1 **13...♖ac8 14.♖fc1 c5! 15.dxc5 ♘xc5**

Yes, Black has an isolated pawn, but this also gives him a space advantage. Things didn't get terribly exciting after this, and the game ended in a draw.

If there is one top player we associate with idiosyncratic opening ideas, it is the Hungarian Richard Rapport. But his approach sometimes backfires, as for instance when he played the Jobava System (1.d4 d5 2.♘c3 ♘f6 3.♗f4 e6 4.♘b5) against Anish Giri.

However, a real opening treat was his first move against Vidit.

Vidit Gujrathi
Richard Rapport
Wijk aan Zee 2019 (12)
Queen's Pawn Game, Chigorin Variation

1.d4 ♘c6!? Now there is real provocation for you! Note that Miles and Short have also moved the steed on move 1. Now the promising Indian grandmaster decided to forego all attempts at refuting 1...♘c6 – which must start with 2.d5 – and went for the solid **2.♘f3!?** Black would be happy after 2.c4 e5 3.d5 ♘ce7, continuing ...♘g6, ...♘f6 and playing his dark-squared bishop to c5 or b4. Play might transpose to certain (fairly decent) lines from the Black Knight's Tango. However, what happens if White goes for it with 2.d5 ♘e5 ?

– Here White has the solid 3.f4 ♘g6 4.e4 e5 (4...e6 5.dxe6 leads to the same position) 5.dxe6! dxe6 (this is safer than 5...fxe6?! 6.♘f3 ♗c5 7.♘c3 ♘f6 8.e5 ♘g4 9.♘e4, as happened for instance in a 2018 internet blitz game Aronian-Caruana) 6.♕xd8+ ♔xd8 7.♘f3, and this is a position that grandmaster Stevic has played repeatedly, with Black with decent results, but in which White nevertheless looks pleasantly better.

– The most normal move is 3.e4 e6 4.f4. This is what refutations look like, and it is indeed the most popular move in the database. However, if Black knows his way, it should, in fact, lead to a draw by force! 4...exd5! This is the point! (In practice Black has far more often played 4...♘g6, when 5.dxe6 once again leads to the position that we are already familiar with.)

5.fxe5 (no improvement is 5.♕xd5 ♘c6 6.♕d1 ♗b4+ 7.c3 ♗c5 8.♕f3 d6 9.♗e3 ♗xe3 10.♕xe3 ♘f6 11.♘d2 0-0 12.0-0-0 ♖e8, Altini-Godena, Turin 2012. However, 5.♘c3!? – Yearbook 125 – deserves attention) 5...♕h4+!. This is it – note that Rapport was familiar with the whole line from his own experience. 6.♔e2 (worse is

6.g3 ♕xe4+ 7.♔e2 ♕xh1 8.♘f3 b6 (Gyimesi-Diebl, Germany 2011), while 6.♔d2 ♕h6+ leads to a perpetual, whichever king move White now decides on, Black has a decent check with his queen) 6...♕h5+ 7.♔d2 ♕h6+ 8.♔c3 ♕c6+ 9.♔d2 ♕h6+.

This is how Black can force a perpetual check. In Erdös-Rapport, Szombathely 2012, Rapport wasn't that easily satisfied and played for a win instead, only to acquiesce in another perpetual on move 27 (after many adventures). So after 3.e4 e6 it is correct to play 4.dxe6 dxe6 (instead, 4...fxe6 5.♘c3 looks rather nice for White) 5.♕xd8+ ♔xd8 when, after 6.f4, Black has the option of going 6...♘c6, as in Gordon-Short, Sheffield 2011.
After 2.♘f3 Rapport transposed to the Chigorin Defence with **2...d5 3.c4 ♗g4 4.♘c3** Instead, 4.cxd5 ♗xf3 5.gxf3 ♕xd5 6.e3 e5 7.♘c3 ♗b4 8.♗d2 ♗xc3 9.bxc3 is one of the main tabiyas of the Chigorin.

Rapport had some experience with this position: 9...♕d6 10.♖b1 0-0-0 (10...b6) 11.♕b3 b6 12.♕xf7 ♔b8 (12...♘f6; 12...♘h6) 13.♕c4 ♕f6 14.♗g2 ♘ge7 15.f4 exf4 16.exf4 ♘a5

17.♕a6 ♕e6+ 18.♔e3? ♘f5 19.0-0 ♘h4! 20.♕b5 ♘xg2 21.f5 (21.♖xa5 ♘xe3! wins for Black!), and now, instead of 21...♕c8 (Hammer-Rapport, Reykjavik 2015), 21...♕c4! 22.♖xa5 ♕xa6 23.♖xa6 ♘h4 would have given Black a large endgame edge. The knight is good, and so is his pawn structure, whereas the white rook on a6 is looking lost.
4...e6 5.e3 A quiet and positional approach that is not critical.
5.cxd5 exd5 6.♗g5 ♗e7 7.♗xe7 ♘gxe7 8.e3 0-0 9.♗e2 ♕d6 occurred twice in Rapport's practice (against Sokolov and Tomashevsky).
5...♘f6 Chigorin used to play 5...♗b4 6.♕b3 ♗xf3 7.gxf3 ♘ge7 with great success against strong opposition.
6.♕b3 ♗xf3 7.gxf3 ♖b8 8.a3N ♗e7 9.f4 0-0 10.♕c2 ♕d7 11.♖g1 ♘a5 12.cxd5 exd5 13.b4

and now, rather than **13...♘c4? 14.♘xd5 ♘xd5 15.♗xc4,** after which Black was clearly worse, Rapport should have played the modest 13...♘c6, when Black has equal chances in a complex position.

If you are not too worried about the queenless middlegame that may arise after 2.d5 ♘e5 3.f4 ♘g6 4.e4 e6 5.dxe6, then this could be a weapon for you. The advantage of the 1...♘c6 move order is that 2.c4 e5 is fairly OK, while 2.♘f3 d5 leads to a particular branch of the Chigorin in which Black has managed to avoid some other lines (3.♘c3 and 3.cxd5 ♕xd5 4.e3).

I hope you have enjoyed our SOS-tour of Wijk aan Zee 2019! ∎

Judit Polgar

Think twice!

Moves often lead to automatic replies, answers that you
don't have to spend time on because they look forced.
That may be a good moment to briefly pause and activate
what **JUDIT POLGAR** calls 'the think-twice filter'.

Learning processes in chess are usually structured in such a way as to allow us to take many decisions intuitively and automatically. This may pertain to opening move orders, methods of treating certain pawn structures or typical elementary tactical operations. While automatic answers help one to save time and energy throughout the game – especially in time-trouble or when anticipating it – it always remains useful to use a 'think-twice filter' in order to avoid bitter surprises.

This is even more apparent when we are thinking of piece or pawn captures and recaptures, or a series of exchanges. For instance, when analysing a position, exchanges like axb4, ...axb4, are usually carried out without much thinking and sometimes even by removing the a-pawns from the board without actually making the moves.

But thinking and acting like this in a practical game can be dangerous, as during this exchanging or recapturing process there may be alternatives available – intermediate moves or checks – that drastically affect the assessment of the position. Even at the highest level, we see situations in which one of the players falls victim

to such automatisms by forgetting to 'think twice'.

One memorable example, which made a deep impression on me at the time, was the following:

Anatoly Karpov
Garry Kasparov
Moscow WC match 1984 (9)

position after 46.b4

White has a pleasant endgame with chances to prove the knight to be 'good' and the enemy bishop to be 'bad'. However, it is not so simple to clear the path for his king, and in all probability Black should be able to hold a draw. Even though this position arose after the adjournment, Kasparov committed a serious error: **46... gxh4?** He obviously had counted on 46.gxh4, when White cannot make further progress (it could be that

mentally he just removed the g-pawns in the manner described above). Instead of this excusable mistake, he should have played 46...♔e6!, maintaining the tension and bringing the king closer to the kingside in order to reduce the effect of the attempt at opening the position with g3-g4.
47.♘g2!!

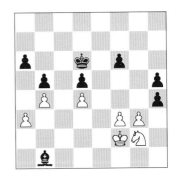

A brilliant (though temporary) pawn sacrifice, after which the king will have a free path to advance.
47...hxg3+ 48.♔xg3 The h5-pawn is doomed, and White has excellent winning chances. Karpov won an instructive (albeit not error-free) endgame.

In fact, as revealed by this game, the 'think twice' issue is related to both opponents. Kasparov forgot about this simple principle, while Karpov surely

'Automatic answers can be dangerous, as there may be alternatives that drastically affect the assessment of the position.'

followed it when he was studying the adjourned position with his seconds!

The same advice applies to the early phase of a combination involving sacrifices. A few years after the previous game, I faced the following situation.

Zirka Frometa
Judit Polgar
Thessaloniki Olympiad 1988

position after 42...♕b7

43.♘xa5? My opponent spent 25 minutes on this move, probably focusing on the variation 43...bxa5 44.♖c7 ♕a8 45.b6, when White has excellent compensation for the piece. But she probably did not 'think twice' about the current position.
On my old score-sheet I found the information that I spent 8 minutes before answering, suggesting that I was taken by surprise. After 'thinking twice' I discovered that I could do better than accepting the sacrifice, even though at first sight the loss of such an important pawn as the one on a5 may seem unacceptable.
43...♕d5!! 44.♕xd5 ♗xd5 45.♘c6?! Analysis showed that 45.♘c4 offered better saving chances.
45...♖e2 The pressure on g2 ensures me an easy win.
46.♖g1 ♖e3! 47.♘b4 g3+ 48.♔h1 ♗e4! Putting the knight under painful domination.

49.♘a2 ♖d3 50.♘c1 ♖d2 51.♘b3 ♖b2 52.♘c1 f5 53.♖e1 ♖xg2 54.♖xe4 ♖h2+ 55.♔g1 fxe4 0-1.

In the next example, White met a more complex sacrifice with a similar queen centralization.

Florin Gheorghiu
Ljubomir Ljubojevic
Manila 1974

position after 22.♘c4

Black is a pawn up, but White has good compensation. Here Ljubojevic was tempted by a seemingly beautiful combination:
22...♖xf2? He must have calculated only the most natural and thematic white answers: 23.♔xf2? ♕xg3+ 24.♔g1 ♘f4, with a huge attack, since White's main pieces are far from the kingside.
And the intermediate 23.d6?, closing the h2-b8 diagonal, surely did not escape his attention, when Black has a second and this time decisive sacrifice: 23...♖xg2+! 24.♔xg2 ♕c6+ 25.♔f2 ♗xh3 26.♖g1 ♕d5, winning. Since Black's last move has taken an important pawn, Ljubojevic obviously thought that White had no alternatives to the lines above.
23.♕e5!
A bolt from the blue! The seemingly passive queen is centralized, forcing the simplification to a winning ending.

23...♕xe5 24.♘xe5 ♗f5 25.♔xf2 ♗xb1 26.d6 Black cannot enjoy his extra pawns, because the d-pawn is very dangerous and his minor pieces are out of play.
26...♔f8 27.♘d7+ ♔e8 28.♘xc5 ♘g7 29.♗xb7 ♘e6 30.♗c6+ ♔d8 31.♘xe6+ fxe6 32.♔e3 e5 33.a5 White's technique in the final phase is very instructive.
33...♗c2 34.g4 g5 35.♗b7 ♔d7 36.♗xa6 ♔xd6 37.♗d3 ♗a4 38.a6 ♔c7 39.♔e4 ♔b6 40.♔xe5 ♗c6 41.♗f1 ♗e8 42.♔f6 h6 43.♔g7 h5 44.♔f6 1-0

Failing to think twice is not always decisive. Sometimes there may be an emergency exit just a few moves later, provided one is able to refrain from the 'automatic' next move.

Here is a highly spectacular recent example.

Denis Khismatullin
Pavel Eljanov
Jerusalem 2015

position after 42.♕h8

Black's king feels uncomfortable, but his passed pawn looks threatening. This must have been Eljanov's consideration when playing his next move.

42...♕c2?! This move has the drawback of taking the queen too far from the king. If he had foreseen White's incredible resource, he would have chosen the safe way with 42...♖xc6, and the game should have ended in a draw.

43. ♕f8+ ♔g5

Black is threatening mate, the d-pawn is strong and f2 is vulnerable. E.g., if 44.♖e1? ♖f6 45.f4+ ♔h4 46.♕h6+ ♔g3 47.♕g5+ ♔h2, the black king reaches safety and the threat ...d3-d2 wins. If 48.♕xf6 ♕xg2 mate. But White found a fantastic move.

44.♔g1!! It is not for nothing that the king's safety is considered the most important criterion in the evaluation system offered by many authors. The white king is heading for h2 while the black one will remain in grave danger. The rook on d6 is hanging, too, the c-pawn is annoying and threats like ♕xf7 and f2-f4 are likely to yield a decisive attack. Clearly a second moment for 'thinking twice'.

44...♕xd1+? If you can take a full rook with check, you hardly consider alternatives. But this leaves the c-pawn unattended, forcing Black to spend an essential tempo to eliminate it.

Black still had a satisfactory defence in the far-from-obvious 44...♖d5!!, with the idea of meeting 45.♕xf7 ♕xd1+ 46.♔h2 with 46...♕f5!, preventing 48.♕f8+ after 47.f4+? ♔h6.

White could try another quiet king move with 45.♔h2, but Black can answer in a similar way with 45...♔f6!!, defending f7, when White would retain some initiative but nothing concrete.

45.♔h2 The white king has not only reached absolute safety, but it also controls g3, which is essential in the mating attack based on f2-f4.

45...♖xc6 46.♕e7+ ♔h6 47.♕f8+ ♔g5 48.♕xf7! Threatening ♕f4+ or f2-f4+, with a mating attack. **48...♖f6 49.f4+ ♔h6 50.♕xf6** The complications have ended and the d-pawn is too slow to counterbalance White's attack. **50...♕e2 51.♕f8+ ♔h5 52.♕g7 h6 53.♕e5+ ♔h4 54.♕f6+ ♔h5 55.f5 gxf5 56.♕xf5+ ♔h4 57.♕g6** 1-0.

I have to end with the warning that 'thinking twice' may sometimes be wrong.

Levon Aronian
Alexander Grischuk
Berlin 2018

position after 28...♕f7

Here Aronian played **29.♕d8+** and the game ended in a draw. Unlike in the previous example, there were no reasons for not taking a piece with check: 29.♕xc8+ ♔h7, and now the simplest human move is 30.♕d7, keeping a decisive material advantage. Doubtlessly, Aronian was tempted to take the bishop, but when double-checking he must have seen some ghosts.

Conclusion

■ Even when the next move (yours or your opponent's) seems to be forced, you should remain alert to unexpected alternatives.

■ In tactical positions, when calculating forcing moves looks essential, you should not discard quiet alternatives. ■

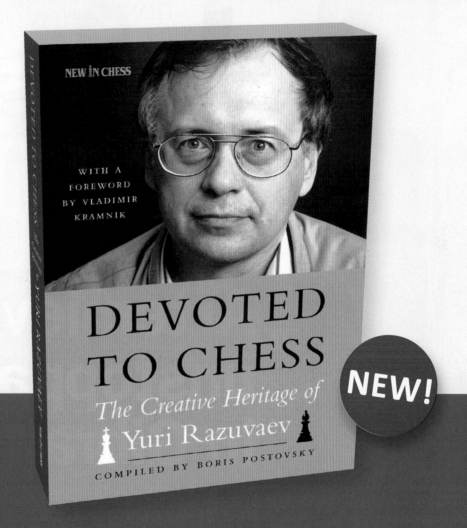

Artemiev unstoppable in Gibraltar

Young Russian celebrates marriage with outstanding performance

Vladislav Artemiev celebrates the biggest success in his career so far, almost frightening Tan Zhongyi, the winner of the highly attractive women's prize.
On the far left, a happy tournament director, Stuart Conquest. On the far right, the moving force behind the Festival, Brian Callaghan.

As the top seeds faltered and fell by the wayside, a rising tide of promising youngsters dominated the Gibraltar Chess Festival. Vladislav Artemiev (20) won seven games and went straight for first place, while runner-up Murali Karthikeyan (19) made everyone forget that he was seeded only 49th! The coveted 'Women's Champion' cheque of £15,000 was claimed by China's Tan Zhongyi. The inimitable **ADHIBAN BASKARAN** reports from the Rock.

T he last time I was in Gibraltar was in 2015, and it was great to return to the Rock. I have lots of happy memories from the past and it was time to create new ones. This time I was able to witness the rising tide of new youngsters, who took centre stage as the elite were given a run for their money!

The Gibraltar Chess Festival is such an attractive tournament, because professionals are playing alongside amateurs and there are so many side events where all of them can mix, which creates a wonderful atmosphere. One that I enjoyed a lot was the exclusive Master Classes, given by Nakamura, Khademalsharieh (one more upcoming player from Iran) and yours truly! They go for roughly one hour and we go through one of our games and also answer lots of interesting questions! One of them was: 'Name a sport other than chess in which you can beat Vishy Anand!' To which I replied: 'Any sport other than chess! ☺' I was put in my place by someone in the audience who retorted: 'I don't think you can beat him in tennis!' Upon which I apologized and told them that I had forgotten about tennis.

And of course one of the major annual highlights is the traditional 'Battle of the Sexes', in which the men's team is headed by our Captain Nigel Short, and the queens are led by Antoaneta Stefanova. We won the first game, but the women came back strongly and won the next two rounds, winning the match. I was one of the main culprits for our third game loss (though, in my defence, I tried to warn Nigel against including me in the team by mentioning that I was in fact supporting the women's team ☺). One hilarious moment was when one of our major stars, David Howell, said: 'I take this feud very seriously and I was preparing myself for this battle!' And then Nigel decided to

'I was able to witness the rising tide of new youngsters, who took centre stage as the elite were given a run for their money!'

ask the question that was on everyone's mind: 'How do you prepare for such a battle?' Howell decided not to elaborate.

The Monster of Gibraltar

It was in 2015 that Hikaru Nakamura decided to play here for the first time, and I think he managed to change the scenario and history of Gibraltar forever! Following his debut, he has won Gibraltar for three consecutive years. I would be tempted to say that he was the first one of the absolute elite (2775 and above, in case you are curious) who decided to play in a Swiss Open... But that first belongs to someone else, and here I would like to pay respect to one of the greatest players of our era, Vladimir Kramnik, who has announced his retirement. It was in the year 2014, at the Tromsø Olympiad, that Kramnik signed on to participate in the Qatar Masters, which changed the status of Opens forever. I think I can safely say that it was due to his contribution that Opens all over the world got a major boost. They became much stronger and many players got a chance to play with the elite, who until then had been playing only in closed events.

Vladimir Kramnik – the only player who managed to beat Garry Kasparov in a match. He has beaten literally all the great players of our era in amazing style. Fantastic opening preparation, clear command of the middle-game and crystal-clear technique were his trademark. If I had to choose my favourite game of his it would be Kasparov-Kramnik, Dos Hermanas 1996. After running into Kasparov's fabled opening prep, Vlad reacted with a stunning piece sacrifice and followed it up with very energetic play, beating Garry at his own game! He will be sorely missed by all of us.

But let's get back to Nakamura. As I had only scored one and a half points in the first two rounds – which is considered a disastrous start in an Open – my only consolation came in the form of Naka and Yu Yangyi, both on 1 out of 2. After some days I met Naka in the lift and he asked me how I was doing and I mentioned that I was on 3½/4. When I asked him the same question, he said 3. I exclaimed, 'So, you are back!', to which he smiled and replied, 'Well, that's the thing about Opens, at some point you always come back!'. That's a good lesson, which neither I nor our readers should forget!

Here's a lesson that he taught in Round 6.

Hikaru Nakamura
Eduardo Iturrizaga
Gibraltar 2019 (6)
Queen's Indian

1.d4 ♘f6 2.c4 e6 3.♘f3 b6 4.g3 ♗b7 5.♗g2 ♗e7 6.0-0 0-0 7.♖e1 ♕c8 8.♘c3 ♘e4 9.♗f4 ♘xc3 10.bxc3 ♗e4

11.♗f1 Time to retreat! The usual plan to get rid of the bishop on e4 without exchanging the Catalan bishop.
11...♗d6 12.♗c1!?
I meant all of them!
12...c5 This is asking for trouble.
13.d5 Now White is clearly better,

because the black bishop on e4 starts feeling uncomfortable.
13...exd5 14.cxd5 ♖e8 15.c4 ♕a6

16.♘d2! Preparing the following exchange sacrifice.
16...♗e5 17.♘xe4 ♗xa1 18.♘d6 ♖f8 19.e4 ♗e5 20.♗f4 ♗xd6
20...f6 21.♗xe5 fxe5 22.♕a1 is also hopeless. The main problem for Black is the Knightmare on d6 ☺!
21.♗xd6 For all the kids: 'Never forget to develop all your pieces'!
21...♖e8 22.e5

A picturesque position showing the domination of the white forces.
22...♕xa2 23.♖e4 Going for the king, which has no protectors left...
23...♘a6 24.♖g4 ♕b2 25.♕f3 ♘b4 26.♕f6 g6

27.h4! Bringing in even more soldiers into the battle. **27...h5 28.♖f4 ♖f8 29.g4** Black resigned. 'A good game for the teachers to show their students!' was how Naka summed up this game.

Newly-wed
The star of this event and the clear winner was Vladislav Artemiev, who clearly demonstrated his superiority. No one was able to stop him on his road towards one of his greatest triumphs after having been married for three months. His main strength seems to be that he avoids mainstream theory and takes the fight to the middlegame, where he is able to switch between dynamic and positional play, depending on the needs of the position. Another interesting trait is defending worse positions, which serves him well, although in Gibraltar he was never in any big trouble.

A key moment was his win in Round 7 against the three-time winner.

Vladislav Artemiev
Hikaru Nakamura
Gibraltar 2019 (7)

position after 17...♗f6

Things have been pretty quiet until now... **18.h3!** All white pieces are ready and hence it was time to step up a gear! **18...♘b4** This doesn't work well, because the knight will be sorely missed. Safer was 18...♖ce8 19.g4 g6, holding the fort, although White can continue with 20.g5 ♗g7 21.h4, with attacking chances along the h-file.
19.g4 g6 20.e4 One of the drawbacks of ...♘b4, since there are no more ...♘d4 ideas.

20...fxe4
The cool-headed 20...♗g7 was probably more stubborn, although White is anyway better after 21.e5.
21.dxe4 ♘xe4
This plays into White's hand. He will now dominate the light squares!
Better was 21...♗d4+ 22.♔h2, when White should be preferred due to his central influence.
22.♘xe4 ♗xb2 23.♘eg5

The e6-pawn will fall, and Black's problems will become unsolvable.
23...♗xf3 24.♖xf3 ♗d4+ 25.♔h1 ♖ce8 26.♘xe6 ♕c6 27.f5 ♕xa4 28.fxg6 ♖xf3 29.gxh7+ ♔h8 30.♗xf3

30...♘c6 Black's last chance was 30...♘d3! 31.♕xd3 (31.♖xd3 ♕xc4

was the key: 32.♖xd4 ♕xe2 33.♗xe2 cxd4 34.♘xd4 ♖e4, winning one of the pieces and leading to a draw) 31...♖xe6, with saving chances due to the opposite-coloured bishops.
31.♘xc5 Black resigned. Somehow Artemiev made it look very easy...

And this is what the 20-year-old Russian did the next day.

Vladislav Artemiev
David Navara
Gibraltar 2019 (9)

position after 19...♗h3

Here Artemiev went for the sexy
20.♕xa7!
The comp feels White should go for

20.♗g2 ♗g4 21.♗f3, with a draw. When will they ever learn?
20...♗xf1 21.♔xf1 Thanks to the exchange sacrifice, White controls the light squares and can hope to break through with a4-a5. Good stuff!
21...♖e7 22.♕a4

The comp gives Black the advantage, but in a practical game it was easier to play with White, and Artemiev won this important game going into the final round with a half point lead.

Artemiev capped his efforts in the final round, where he faced Yu Yangyi with the black pieces. A draw would probably yield him a tie for first and a tiebreak, while a win would obviously settle the matter right away.

Three-time winner Hikaru Nakamura could not fight for first place this year, but that did not stop him from having a good time.

NOTES BY
Vladislav Artemiev

Yu Yangyi
Vladislav Artemiev
Gibraltar 2019 (10)
Caro-Kann Defence, Advance Variation

1.e4 c6
For this last-round game I chose the Caro-Kann Defence – a solid opening and at the same time a very complicated one.
2.d4 d5 3.e5 ♗f5 4.♘f3 e6 5.♗e2 ♘d7
Another possibility is 5...c5, after which there is a great deal of theory.
6.0-0 ♗g6

This solid line for Black has a contradictory reputation. On the one hand, Black's position is very flexible: the knight from g8 can quickly reach the good square f5, and then, as a rule, Black endeavours to play solid, positional chess, not forcing events. If White acts in the same manner, Black gradually prepares ...c5, and it may transpire that the knight on f5 is ideally placed – White's d4-point is very vulnerable. The drawback to the variation is that Black plays unhurriedly, and if White acts energetically and enterprisingly, Black sometimes encounters concrete problems.
7.c3
For the moment White avoids deciding where to place his b1-knight. The main continuation here is 7.♘bd2. White also plays 7.a4 or 7.b3.
7...♘h6 8.a4
After 8.♗xh6 gxh6, Black's pawn structure is seriously damaged, but on the other hand he has two good

DAVID LLADA / GIBRALTAR CHESS FESTIVAL

bishops and possible undermining moves – ...c5 or ...f6. In my view the position is roughly equal, a kind of dynamic balance.

8...a5!? If 8...♘f5, then 9.a5 a6 10.b4 and, frankly speaking, the black player may experience a certain depression – because if he simply stands still, there is a great risk of getting totally squeezed, while if he attempts to find counterplay (via the move ...f6), Black will acquire a new weakness – the pawn on e6, and the e5-point will be happily occupied by a white piece. The games Caruana-Bareev (2016, 1-0) and Fedoseev-Vitiugov (2016, 1-0) are very instructive.

9.♘a3 ♗e7 10.♘c2 0-0 11.♘ce1

11...c5 It is hard to get by without this undermining move. White now has the b5-square, but this is not very dangerous for Black.

12.♗xh6 Evidently the correct decision. Otherwise Black has no problems: 12.♘d3 cxd4 (or 12...♖c8).

12...gxh6 13.♗b5 cxd4 14.cxd4
In the event of 14.♗xd7 ♕xd7 15.♘xd4 the position is complicated, but Black's chances in the forthcoming play are not worse. The two bishops compensate for the slight defect in his pawn structure; also there is the c4-square for a rook and in the future it may be possible to create play on the queenside with ...b5. But White also does not experience any difficulties: he has control of d4 and the plan with f4-f5. The position is roughly equal.

Remaining cool and collected till the very last day, Vladislav Artemiev confidently waited for his counter-chances against Yu Yangyi.

24...h5! An accurate move; Black is alright. Bad is 24...♘b4? 25.♘g4 ♘xd3 26.♘xg6!.

25.g4
A risky move, although permissible. After 25.♗e2 ♕c2 26.♘xh5+ ♗xh5 (26...♔h8!? is interesting) 27.♗xh5 ♕xd2 28.♖xd2 ♘c1!?, Black has sufficient compensation for the pawn.
25...♘b4 A practical decision, as other options seemed very unclear.

26.♗xg6
As 26.♘xh5+ ♗xh5 27.gxh5 ♘xd3 28.♕xd3 ♕c2 gives White nothing. An alternative to the move in the game was the variation 26.♘xg6 fxg6!? 27.gxh5 ♘xd3 28.h6+ ♔f8 29.♕xd3 ♕c2, or 26...hxg6 27.gxh5 gxh5 28.♗b1.
26...hxg6 27.gxh5 ♕c2 28.hxg6 ♕f5!
An important move (I saw it when I played 25...♘b4).

29.♕e3?! With this move the collapse of White's position begins. 29.gxf7 was essential, when the position remains unclear, although roughly equal.
29...fxg6 30.♕g3 30.♘g2 ♖c2.
30...♖f8 31.♘g2

14...♘b8!? A good positional decision.
15.♕d2 ♔g7 16.♘d3 ♘a6 17.♘f4 ♕b6 When I made this move I saw that I was allowing the plan with h4, but I wanted to play my rook from c8 to f8 and return my queen to d8, which looks harmonious. The alternative was 17...♖c8.
18.h4!? ♖fc8 19.♖fc1 ♖xc1+ 20.♖xc1 ♘b4

21.g3! A strong move, over which my opponent, if I remember correctly, thought for rather a long time.
21...♘a2 With this move Black indicates that he is not averse to a draw by repetition. On the whole, by the position this is justified. And by the tournament situation – even more so.
22.♖d1 The opponent is aggressively inclined – which is understandable, this being a battle for victory in the tournament.
22...♖c8 23.♘h2
The positional 23.♘e1 would have continued the unhurried play. Possibly White is even a touch better, but Black is very solidly placed.
23...♕c7 24.♗d3
24.♘g4?! was dubious in view of 24...♕c2 with the initiative, for example: 24.♘xg6 hxg6 25.♘g4 ♖h8 (but not 25...g5? 26.hxg5 hxg5 27.♗d3 ♘b4 28.♗b1 with an attack) 26.♖a1 ♘b4 27.♖c1 ♕d8.

31...♕c2 Interesting, and perhaps more accurate, was 31...♕c6!?, followed by the transfer of the bishop to b6. Black has a positional advantage and a comfortable position.

32.♘e3? A weak move. Correct was 32.♖f1! ♘c6 (32...♕e4 33.♖e1, when 33...♕xd4? 34.♘f3 is not possible) 33.♕g4.

32...♕e4?! This move suggests itself, but it could have allowed White to correct his mistake. 32...♕e2 was strong, when Black has an enormous positional advantage. Things are very difficult for White.

33.♘eg4?

The only move was 33.♘g2. After 33...♗d8 Black is better, but for the moment White is not lost.

33...♘c6 Black is almost winning. Perhaps simply winning.

34.♕e3 ♖f4 35.♘f6 ♗xf6 36.exf6+ ♔xf6 37.♕xe4

It was better to try 37.♕a3, although also in this case Black has a winning position, e.g. 37...♔g7 38.f3 ♕e2 39.♖f1 ♘xd4 40.♕e7+ ♖f7 41.♕g5 ♕xb2 42.♕e5+ ♔h7 43.♔h1 ♕d2 and Black wins.

37...♖xe4 38.♘f3 ♘e7

The simplest. The rook ending with an extra pawn and the weakness on d4 is easily won for Black.

39.♔g2?! A little more resilient was 39.♖b1! ♘f5 40.b4 b6 41.bxa5 bxa5 42.♖b5 ♖f4! 43.♖e1 (43.♘h2 ♖xd4 44.♖xa5 ♘xh4, and Black wins) 43...♖xd4 44.♖xa5 ♖d1 45.♔f1 ♘d4 with a won endgame for Black.

39...♘f5 40.♖d3 ♘xh4+ 41.♘xh4 ♖xh4 42.♔g3 g5 43.♔g2 ♖e4 44.♔g3 ♔f5 45.♔g2 g4 46.♔f1
Or 46.♔g3 ♖e1 47.f3 gxf3 48.♔xf3 ♖h1! 49.♔g2 ♔e4 and Black wins.

46...b6

The conversion proceeds seamlessly. Black endeavours not to give White even the slightest chance of escaping.

47.♔g2 ♖e1! 48.b3 ♔e4 49.♖d2
Black also wins after 49.♖c3 ♖xd4 50.♖c6 e5 51.♖xb6 ♔c3 or 49.♖g3 ♔xd4 50.♖xg4+ ♔c3 51.♖g3+ ♔c2.

49...♖b1 50.♔g3 ♔f5 51.♖d3 ♖h1 52.♔g2 ♖h3
White resigned.

Perfect finish

Another dark horse who you might say made his international breakthrough was young Murali Karthikeyan. The 19-year-old Indian made

Gibraltar 2019

				TPR
1	Vladislav Artemiev	RUS	2709	8½	2941
2	Murali Karthikeyan	IND	2570	8	2747
3	Nikita Vitiugov	RUS	2720	7½	2779
4	David Howell	ENG	2685	7½	2705
5	David Anton	ESP	2642	7½	2696
6	David Navara	CZE	2738	7	2790
7	Nils Grandelius	SWE	2682	7	2771
8	Lalith Babu M R	IND	2547	7	2767
9	Le Quang Liem	VIE	2714	7	2741
10	Ivan Saric	CRO	2690	7	2736
11	Wesley So	USA	2765	7	2734
12	Yu Yangyi	CHN	2764	7	2715
13	Maxime Vachier-Lagrave	FRA	2780	7	2708
14	Michael Adams	ENG	2701	7	2706
	Kirill Alekseenko	RUS	2637	7	2706
16	Hikaru Nakamura	USA	2749	7	2703
17	Romain Edouard	FRA	2643	7	2692
18	Rauf Mamedov	AZE	2703	7	2681
19	Pavel Eljanov	UKR	2680	7	2673
20	Hrant Melkumyan	ARM	2660	7	2659
21	Maxim Matlakov	RUS	2700	7	2642
22	Tan Zhongyi	CHN	2502	7	2585
23	Mariya Muzychuk	UKR	2540	6½	2718
24	Levon Aronian	ARM	2767	6½	2706
25	Suri Vaibhav	IND	2590	6½	2685
26	Maxime Lagarde	FRA	2604	6½	2652
27	Gukesh D	IND	2497	6½	2650
28	Adhiban Baskaran	IND	2689	6½	2637
29	Rinat Jumabayev	KAZ	2604	6½	2636
30	Ivan Cheparinov	GEO	2691	6½	2635
31	Akshat Chandra	USA	2492	6½	2634
32	Gawain Jones	ENG	2691	6½	2629
33	Mikhail Antipov	RUS	2589	6½	2626
34	Daniel Sadzikowski	POL	2534	6½	2617
35	Daniil Yuffa	RUS	2578	6½	2601
36	Evgeniy Solozhenkin	RUS	2427	6½	2586
37	Jules Moussard	FRA	2605	6½	2582
38	Aryan Tari	NOR	2625	6½	2561
39	Alexander Donchenko	GER	2604	6½	2557
40	Buhl Bjerre Jonas	DEN	2422	6½	2511
41	Arkadij Naiditsch	AZE	2734	6	2654
42	Rasmus Svane	GER	2594	6	2648
43	Bogdan-Daniel Deac	ROU	2603	6	2643
44	Jose Cuenca	ESP	2512	6	2637
45	Ju Wenjun	CHN	2575	6	2608
46	Dennes Abel	GER	2458	6	2607
47	Harsha Bharathakoti	IND	2481	6	2601
48	Jan Werle	NED	2541	6	2600
49	Humpy Koneru	IND	2541	6	2595
50	Abhimanyu Puranik	IND	2536	6	2595
252 players, 10 rounds					

his grand debut in Gibraltar with a clear second place, winning his last five games, three of them against 2700+ opposition! Karthi is well-known in Indian circles. He was U12 World Champion and won the National title twice, with Vidit there. I also played in one of them.

Karthi had an important wake-up moment in Round 5, when he faced off against Nakamura.

Murali Karthikeyan
Hikaru Nakamura
Gibraltar 2019 (5)

position after 18...e6

19.♗e4 The first step in the wrong direction. 19.♕g2! would have kept control, with a clear advantage to White thanks to the two bishops and more space.
19...♖ae8 Already Naka is preparing the following blow, which Karthi had possibly missed/underestimated.
20.♕d3 The funny return with 20.♗c2! was one of the few ways to maintain the advantage.
20...f5!

Naka had been waiting his entire life for this blow!!

21.♗f3 After 21.gxf6 ♘xf6 22.dxe6 ♘xe4 23.♕xe4 ♕e7, Black is spoiled for choice, but White can hold quite easily with 24.♕d5 ♕xe6 25.♗c1 due to the reduced material.
21...♘xf4! 22.♗xf4 e5

And Naka brought home the point convincingly.

This loss left Karthi quite upset. How could he botch up such a nice position? Little did he know that the event was only beginning for him! I think the most suitable quote here would be: 'You can either let the one loss define you... Or you can learn from it!' And this is exactly what he did. He was pretty much unstoppable in the next five rounds! Karthi set the scene for a dramatic last day in the penultimate round.

Murali Karthikeyan
Maxim Matlakov
Gibraltar 2019 (9)

position after 16...♘gf6

Matlakov hasn't exactly fought against White's setup, and now Karthi further increases White's influence.

Magnus Carlsen: 'Karthikeyan is a good, solid player, but you don't expect him just to outplay Maxime like this, so it's very, very impressive'

17.♘h4! ♘c5 **18.f3** 18.♘g6 was stronger. **18...d5** 18...b5! was the right break: 19.axb5 axb5 20.♖xa8 ♗xa8 21.♗xb5 ♘fxe4 22.fxe4 ♗xh4, with an interesting middlegame.
19.exd5 ♘xd5 20.♘f5
Now Black is under lots of pressure.
20...♗f6 21.♖fd1 ♘xc3 22.♗xc3 ♕c7 23.♘d6 ♗c6 24.♗xe5

And just like that, White achieved a winning position!

Before we take a look at the epic final-round clash between Karthi and Maxime Vachier-Lagrave, here's a quote from none other than the current World Champion during the live broadcast on Chess24: 'And I see that Maxime is dead lost... he was a bit worse early on, but you don't expect him to just go down in flames... I've liked [Karthikeyan's] game for a while – a good, solid player, but you don't expect him just to outplay Maxime like this, so it's very, very impressive.'

NOTES BY
Murali Karthikeyan

**Murali Karthikeyan
Maxime Vachier-Lagrave**
Gibraltar 2019 (10)
Sicilian Defence, Najdorf Variation

The night before the last round, I was really nervous and unable to sleep properly because of the thoughts about this game against the top seed. As my friends Vaibhav and Lalith pointed out, I should go for a safe and risk-free line, but the game went completely differently! With 16...♖g8, Black threw away all his chances, and when he didn't play correctly in a slightly worse endgame, I slowly improved and won. Somehow I couldn't believe it when the position was turning into my favour.

1.e4 c5 2.♘f3 d6 3.d4 cxd4 4.♘xd4 ♘f6 5.♘c3 a6 The Najdorf, of course. **6.♗e3 ♘g4 7.♗g5 h6 8.♗h4 g5 9.♗g3 ♗g7 10.♗e2**
To be honest, while I played 10.♗e2, I realized that I had not looked at the 10...h5 line. And he played that!

10...h5 11.h4 ♘c6
Here, I took a lot of time to decide between three knight moves.

12.♘f3?! The correct way to fight for an advantage is 12.♘b3 gxh4 13.♗xh4 ♗e6 14.♕d2 ♖c8 15.f3 ♗h6 16.♗g5 ♗xg5 17.♕xg5 ♘f6 18.♕d2 ♖g8 19.♗f1. MVL himself has played this as White.
12.♘xc6 bxc6 13.hxg5 ♖b8 14.♕d2 ♖xb2 15.♘d1 ♖b8 is just equal.

12...gxh4 13.♗xh4
Basically, if White gets ♘d5 and c3, he will be clearly better. Black should react immediately.

13...♕a5 I expected Black not to go for 13...♗e6 14.♘d5 ♗xb2 15.♖b1 ♕a5+ 16.♔f1 ♕xa2 17.♘c7+, when I think I have some counterplay.

14.♕d2
I felt I should not swap my knight and pawn against his bishop with 14.0-0 ♗xc3 15.bxc3 ♕xc3, because my h4-bishop is not doing anything.

14...♗e6 15.♖d1
15.0-0 ♖c8 16.♖ab1 was an interesting option, but I wanted to release the tension on c3.

15...♖c8 After 15...♖g8!? I was planning to play 16.♘d5 ♗xd5 17.♕xa5 ♖xa5 18.♖xd5 ♗xb2 19.0-0. As the game went on, I felt that I had many ideas with at least equality!

16.0-0

16...♖g8? I didn't understand this move. Black has lots of moves that give at least equality. After, e.g., 16...♗xc3 17.bxc3 ♘ce5, I felt Black is better because I have very few ideas here and I cannot afford to go into any type of pawn-down endgames. And after 16...♕b4!? 17.♘d5 ♕xe4 I can't say Black is better, because of the king on e8.

17.♘d5 ♕xd2 18.♖xd2 ♗h6?!
I don't think Black is much worse after 18...♗xd5 19.exd5 ♘ce5 20.♘xe5 ♗xe5.

19.♖dd1 f6 20.c3 I was sure I was not worse here, but I didn't feel I had an advantage (honestly!). Still, I wondered why Black went for this.

20...♗g5?!
20...♔f7!? 21.♗g3 ♘e3 22.♘xe3 ♗xe3 23.♗xd6 exd6 24.fxe3 looked like a good practical try.

21.♗g3 ♗h6?
Better was 21...♖h8 22.♘xg5 fxg5 23.f3 ♘ge5 24.♗f2, although White is obviously better. I can understand that landing from a position with chances of ∓ to a ± position is not easy to accept, but one has to play according to the position.

22.♘h4

Now I was sure I had a very clear advantage, because Black had wasted two moves, ...♝g5 and back, while White improved his pieces.

22...♚f7 22...♞ce5!? 23.♞f5 ♝f8 24.c4 is just better for White.

23.♞f5 ♝xf5 24.exf5

Now White is clearly better. But I didn't feel yet that I was winning!

24...♜g5 25.♝c4

Bad was 25.♝f4? ♜xf5 26.♝xg4 hxg4 27.♝xh6 ♜h8 28.♝f4 (28.♝e3?? ♜fh5 29.f4 g3 and mate!) 28...e6 29.f3 ♜xd5, and Black will save the draw. This is not how you want a good position to end.

25...♞a5 After 25...♞ce5, White has 26.♝b3, followed by ♞f4.

26.♝d3

26...♜cg8 Interesting was 26...♞e5!? 27.♜fe1 ♜cg8 28.♝e4 ♜xg3 29.fxg3 ♜xg3 30.♚f2 h4, with some chances to hold.

27.♝f4

27.f4 ♜5g7 28.♝h4 would have been cool. Black doesn't have a place for his g4-knight and h6-bishop to move to.

27...♜5g7 28.♜fe1 ♞c6

After 28...♞e5 29.♝xh6 ♜xg2+ 30.♚f1 Black won't have anything.

The plan was to go for a safe and risk-free line, but after the opening it began to dawn on Murali Karthikeyan that there were chances to beat Maxime Vachier-Lagrave.

29.♝e4 Tempting was 29.♝c4!? ♞ge5 30.♝b3 ♜xg2+ 31.♚h1, but I felt that I didn't need to go for this variation when I had so many options for a simple advantage.

29...h4 29...♜h8!? 30.♝xh6 ♞xh6 31.♞f4, and White is winning.

30.f3

Here I was sure that I was winning.

30...♝xf4

30...♞ge5!? was a good practical try, although White should prevail after 31.♝xh6 ♜xg2+ 32.♚h1 ♜2g3 33.♞f4 ♜h8 34.♞e2 ♜xh6 35.♞xg3 hxg3+ 36.♚g2 ♜h2+ 37.♚xg3 ♜xb2 38.f4 ♞d7 39.♝d5+ ♚f8 40.♜h1, and wins. Of course, I saw all this.

31.♞xf4 ♞ge5 32.♝d5+ ♚e8

33.♝xg8

33.♚f2 ♜h8 34.♜h1, with a winning position, was an alternative if 33.♝xg8 had not worked. Honestly, I couldn't control my nerves and wanted to play 33.♚f2, but I was confident that I was getting a piece with a better position after 33.♝xg8.

33...♘xf3+ After 33...♖xg8 34.♔f2 White is an exchange up.
34.♔f2 ♘xe1 35.♗d5

35...♖g5 After 35...♘c2 36.♖c1 ♖g5 37.♗e6 ♖g4 38.♘g6 White is winning and the f5-pawn is safe. And after 35...♖g4 36.♘e6 Black won't get the annoying f5-pawn either.
36.♔xe1 ♖xf5 37.♘g6 ♖h5 38.♖d3
I wanted to prevent the exchange of the h4-pawn for the g2-pawn.
38...♖h6 39.♘f4 e5 40.♘e6 ♘e7

41.♗xb7 41.♗e4 ♔d7 42.♘g7!? should also win, but I was in no mood to play slow chess!
41...♔d7 42.♘f8+

42...♔c7?!

When I played 41.♗xb7, I wasn't even sure if I would be winning after 42...♔e8 43.♖xd6 ♔f8 44.♖xa6 ♔f7 45.a4 h3 46.gxh3 ♖xh3 47.a5, but Black's problem is that he cannot get behind White's a-pawn easily.
43.♗xa6 d5 44.c4 f5
44...d4 loses to 45.♖b3. And 44...♖h8 to 45.cxd5.
45.♗b5 f4 46.♖a3

And Black resigned. His position is lost; for example: 46...♔b7 47.♘d7 e4 48.♘c5+ ♔b8 49.♖a6 ♖xa6 50.♘xa6+ ♔a7 51.c5, and wins.

The Iceman

One of the regulars in Gibraltar is the 'Iceman', Nikita Vitiugov, who earned this nickname from commentator Simon Williams when he defended a worse position and won the tiebreak and with it the 2013 edition. Six years on, he is still swindling his way...

Nikita Vitiugov
Tan Zhongyi
Gibraltar 2019 (3)

position after 29...♖d6

White is in serious trouble due to his weak d-pawn, so he decides to change the scenario with an interesting pawn sacrifice.
30.f5! ♕xf5 30...gxf5 was the right move, but without a comp it does look dangerous: 31.♕h6 ♕xd4 32.♕xh5+ ♔e7, and apparently the black king can run to the queenside.
31.♖e2! White has passed on the danger baton to Black, who now has to be precise in order to survive; not an easy thing to do when you were better just one move ago!
After 31.♔g1 ♕d5 the check on d4 would have been troublesome.

31...♕g4 The cool-headed 31...♔g7! would have led to 32.♖f2 ♕d5 33.♕f4 ♖d7 34.♕f8+ ♔h7 35.♖f7+, with a perpetual.
32.♖f2+ ♔e7 33.♖f4! ♕d1+ 34.♔h2

Winter (I mean ♕e5) is coming!!
34...♖d5 35.♕a3+ c5 36.♕xa7
The difference between the safety of the kings led to victory for White (1-0, 43).

A normal turn of events for the Iceman... Luckily for her, the former Women's World Champion managed to put this loss behind her and ended up winning the highly coveted 'Women's Champion' prize, worth £15,000 (Artemiev won £25,000, Karthikeyan £20,000). The special women's prizes in Gibraltar are another attraction, and it's small wonder that so many strong ladies participate every year.

Tan Zhongyi collected her biggest scalp in the penultimate round.

Tan Zhongyi
Sebastien Mazé
Gibraltar 2019 (9)
King's Indian, Makagonov System

1.d4 ♘f6 2.c4 g6 3.♘c3 ♝g7 4.e4 d6 5.h3 0-0

6.♝e3!? One of the recent trends against the KID.
6...c5 I tried 6...♘a6 and barely managed to salvage a draw against Caruana in Wijk aan Zee last year. Possibly the only attempt which is giving good results is 6...e5, as was checked in the same event in the game Caruana-Jones.
7.♘f3 cxd4 8.♘xd4 b6 9.g3!

An interesting idea, fianchettoing the bishop, after which Black will find it hard to create any counterplay.

Our man-on-the-spot, Adhiban Baskaran, was not entirely satisfied with his score (6½/10), but no one is going to spoil AD's mood!

9...♝b7 10.♝g2 ♘bd7 11.0-0 ♖b8 12.♕c2 a6 13.a4! h5 14.b3

Black had no play left and had to throw in the towel after 29 moves!
14...e6 15.♖ad1 ♕e7 16.♝g5 ♖fc8 17.f4 e5 18.♘de2 exf4 19.♝xf4 ♘e8 20.♘d4 ♘c7 21.♕f2 ♘e5 22.♘d5 ♘xd5 23.exd5 ♖c7 24.♔h2 a5 25.♖fe1 h4 26.gxh4 ♝f6 27.h5 ♖f8 28.♘f3 ♖c5 29.♕g3
Black resigned.

Chess as Art

One of Kramnik's favourite expressions is 'Chess is an art!'. He has also said that you always need two players

to create a masterpiece, and this is what the following two gentlemen were keenly aware of.

Gawain Jones
Alejandro Ramirez
Gibraltar 2019 (4)
French Defence, Rubinstein Variation

1.e4 e6 2.d4 d5 3.♘d2 dxe4 4.♘xe4 ♘d7 5.♘f3 ♘gf6 6.♘xf6+ ♘xf6 7.g3 b6 8.♝b5+ ♝d7 9.a4 a6 10.♝e2 ♝c6 11.0-0 ♘d7 12.♝c4 ♝e7 13.d5

13...exd5
Here normal people would play 14.♝xd5 and hope for a lasting pull. But Jones wasn't one of them ☺.

14.♘d4!?
Enter the dragon! 14.♗xd5 is for the faint-hearted.
14...♗b7 15.♘f5
And here normal people would play 15...♗f6 and hope to defend a slightly inferior position. But not Ramirez!

15...dxc4
15...♗f6 16.♗xd5 ♗xd5 17.♕xd5 ♘e5, with good chances to neutralize White's pressure.
16.♘xg7+ ♔f8 17.♗h6

17...♔g8 Another pretty way was 17...♘e5!? 18.♘e6+ (18.♘f5+ ♔g8 19.♖e1! f6 20.♕h5 ♗c5 21.♖xe5 fxe5 22.♖d1 looks dangerous but it's the usual 0. 00 after 22...♕e8) 18...♘e8 19.♘xd8 ♘f3+ 20.♔h1 ♖xd8 21.♕c1 ♖g8, with full compensation.
18.♖e1 The usual 'Bring all your pieces' motto turns out to be wrong here. 18.♘e6 fxe6 19.♕g4+ ♔f7 20.♕h5+ is a nice perpetual.
18...♗f8 19.♖e8 ♕f6 20.♖xd7 ♖xe8 21.♘xe8 ♕xh6 22.♕g4+

22...♕g6
Black could have got the advantage with 22...♗g7! 23.♖d1 ♕g6 24.♖d8. I assume both players stopped here... 24...♗e5!. This is totally a computer solution and possibly only for someone with no emotions to find it ☺. 25.♕d7 h6!, and Black untangles by giving back the piece.
23.♘f6+ ♔g7 24.♘e8+
Draw. A fantastic game, for which both of them were awarded the beauty prize!

Struggling Elite

Looking at the games and the results, you have to conclude that the elite players had a hard time in Gibraltar this year. Many must have thought that players like MVL, Wesley So, Levon Aronian or Hikaru Nakamura would fight for first place, but in the end they all had to settle for more modest places. Instead, we saw a rising tide of youngsters and the elite had a hard time coping up with them.

At 28, David Howell is no longer a real youngster, but with his excellent 4th place the Englishman had every reason to be satisfied.

Levon Aronian
David Howell
Gibraltar 2019 (10)
Caro-Kann, Exchange Variation

**1.e4 c6 2.d4 d5 3.exd5 cxd5
4.♗d3 ♘c6 5.c3 ♕c7 6.h3**

6...g6!?

Howell deviates from a previous game, in which he played 6...e5. Maybe Aronian was only expecting this?

After 6...♘f6, 7.♘f3 g6 8.♕c2 has been used successfully by Lev in rapid/blitz formats. I guess he thought the lines were similar.

7.♕c2

Aimed against ...♗f5, but Black meets this idea in a novel way!

Either 7.♘e2, which is the recommendation of Sopiko's Chess24 DVD, or the natural 7.♘f3 would have been preferable.

7...f6! An epic idea, which refutes White's concept.

Images that were viewed countless times on YouTube. Hikaru Nakamura cannot suppress his amazement as he sees what Levon Aronian is doing in this last game against David Howell.

8.♘e2 e5 9.0-0 ♘ge7

Black is never able to create such an impressive centre so soon in this line.

10.dxe5

10.♕a4 ♗d7 is also nice for Black, but with chances for both sides after 11.dxe5 fxe5 12.♘a3.

10...fxe5

Black is already slightly more equal.

11.c4

I was just passing by when Lev played this move and I thought David was in big trouble. How wrong I was!

11...e4 I wonder what Lev had actually missed.

12.♗xe4

12.cxd5 exd3 13.♕xd3 ♘e5 doesn't yield any compensation either.

12...dxe4 13.♘bc3 ♗g7 14.♘d5 ♕d6 15.♗f4 ♗e5!

This is what Lev had missed, but 15...♘e5 was equally strong...

16.♖ad1 ♗xf4 17.♘dxf4 ♕e5

And the rest would be better explained by Naka! You should really check out his hilarious expressions (uploaded on YouTube) after the piece sac, during which David had difficulty concentrating and suppressing his laughter ☺ (0-1, 29). ∎

Cornered queens

Your queen goes after material gains, but strays into a corner. Was it worth it?

Viktor Kupreichik
Lev Alburt
Dubna 1970

1.e4 e6 2.d4 d5 3.e5 c5 4.c3 ♞c6 5.♞f3 ♛b6 6.♗e2 ♞h6 7.♗xh6 ♛xb2 8.♗e3 ♛xa1 9.♛c2 cxd4 10.♞xd4 ♗d7 11.0-0 ♞xe5

Black has incarcerated his queen on a1, but has bagged an exchange and two pawns in return. Basically, White has three choices to profit from such a cornered queen: 1. Restore some sort of material balance and prove your queen will outclass your opponent's pieces; 2. Try and catch the trapped queen in the corner; 3. Just ignore the cornered queen and make use of your surplus elsewhere on the board. **12.♛b3** Going for the king instead of the queen. Kupreichik was not the man to let material prevail over initiative! Meanwhile, the alternatives were not bad. The obvious 12.♞d2 would win the black queen right away, but how to assess the position after 12...♛xf1+ 13.♔xf1, when the material balance is almost equal, but White's lead

in development looks frightening? The second obvious choice was the backward move 12.♞b3, which would catch the queen immediately, if Black did not have 12...♗a4. Still, White seems to be on top here, too, after 13.♗b5+! ♛xb5 14.♞xa1 ♗xf1 15.♔xf1. **12...♞c4** Practically forced. White has not just attacked the b7-pawn, but he had also sneakily vacated the c2-square for another backward knight move... **13.♗xc4 dxc4 14.♛xb7** 14.♛c2, followed by ♞d2, was objectively stronger. **14...♜d8** Sure, 14...♜c8 15.♜d1 seems like asking for trouble. Yet it turns out that the cool 15...♗d6! 16.♞c2 ♛xa2 17.♜xd6 0-0! could have killed White's initiative and allowed Black to gain the upper hand. **15.♞c6 ♗xc6 16.♛xc6+ ♜d7**

17.♜d1? Here White should have completed development with the intermediate 17.♞a3 ♛b2 (17...♛xf1+ 18.♔xf1 ♗xa3 19.♛a8+ ♜d8 20.♛xa7 leaves White on top too) 18.♞b5!, with ample play for the exchange. Soon after the text-

move, which leaves the b1-knight out of play, White started drifting and went on to even lose the game. **17...♗d6 18.♗g5 f6 19.♗f4?** He should have continued 19.♛c8+ ♜d8 20.♛xe6+ ♗e7 21.♜e1 ♜d7 22.♗f4. **19...e5** 0-1, 62.

On the basis of this game (despite White's eventual loss) you might conclude that an exchange is too small a catch to endanger your queen so recklessly. What about winning a full rook?

Igor Zaitsev
Yuri Gutop
Moscow 1992

1.e4 e6 2.d4 d5 3.♞c3 ♗b4 4.♗d3 c5 5.exd5 ♛xd5 6.♗d2 ♗xc3 7.♗xc3 cxd4 8.♗xd4 ♛xg2 9.♛d2!? ♛xh1 10.0-0-0 The immediate 10.f3 leaves Black more room for alternatives, for example 10...♞c6 11.0-0-0 ♞xd4 12.♗b5+ ♗d7! (12...♔f8 13.♛xd4, and already Black is in trouble! His queen will be missed in the defence) 13.♗xd7+ ♔f8 14.♛xd4 ♛xh2, and with Black's queen escaping, White will be struggling with his material deficits. **10... f6 11.f3**

The queen is trapped. Can it be caught, too? **11...♞c6 12.♗c5 ♔f7** 12...♞ge7 looks more natural. **13.♛e2** Indeed, White can always protect the f3-pawn in some way and then win the queen by developing the g1-knight. But the ensuing moves yield Black a solid position. **13...♞ge7 14.♞h3 ♛xd1+ 15.♛xd1**

'You will need to keep a cool head when facing the various dangers that a cornered queen brings about.'

15...e5? So much for solidity. Black should have completed development before opening up the position. **16.f4** First 16.♗c4+ was a valid alternative. **16...♗e6 17.♕f3 ♖ad8?** This just loses material after White's logical follow-up **18.fxe5** After **18...♘xe5 19.♘g5+** Black resigned, since 20.♕xb7 is next. 1-0.

Clearly Black could have put up more of a struggle. Here is a more straightforward example. Less material for the side with the stranded queen; same cage though.

Zhao Jun
Nguyen Anh Dung
Hyderabad 2005

1.d4 ♘f6 2.c4 e6 3.♘c3 ♗b4
4.♕c2 d5 5.cxd5 exd5 6.♗g5 h6
7.♗xf6 ♕xf6 8.e3 0-0 9.a3 ♗f5
10.♗d3 ♗xc3+ 11.bxc3

Do you spot a clever move? **11...♕g6** Yes, tempting, but a grave error! **12.♗xf5 ♕xg2 13.f3!** This little move again keeps the Black queen locked. **13...♕xh1 14.0-0-0** Black

is only an exchange up and soon will have to give up his queen for the rook. He duly lost after **14...g6 15.♘h3 ♘c6 16.♕f2 ♘a5 17.♖f1 ♘c4 18.♘e2 ♕xf1+ 19.♗xf1** 1-0 in 37.

One more similar catch, from a match at the 2012 Women's Olympiad between Bulgaria and China.

Margarita Voiska
Ju Wenjun
Istanbul Olympiad 2012

position after 19.f3

For the moment, a materially equal position! Black's next, however, is too materialistic and grants White the necessary time to catch the queen on h1. **19...♗xf8?** 19...e4! would have disturbed White's plans and favoured Black. **20.♕e2 e4** Too late. **21.0-0-0** And with White's rook participating, the catch is easy. **21...♘g7 22.♖f1 ♖e8 23.f4 ♘f5 24.♘h3** And Ju Wenjun could not escape defeat. **24...♕f3 25.♖xf3 exf3 26.♕d3!** 1-0, 41.

In our last example, Black first launches a small initiative and only then focusses on the queen on a8.

Spyridon Skembris
Boris Gulko
Beer-Sheva 1993

1.d4 d6 2.♘f3 ♗g4 3.e4 ♘f6
4.h3 ♗h5 5.♕e2 e6 6.♗g5 ♗e7
7.♗xf6 ♗xf3 8.♕b5+ c6 9.♕xb7
♗xf6

A tough one: can you safely grab on a8 or would you prefer to take back on f3 first? The answer is below. First the game continuation. **10.♕xa8** 10.gxf3!? ♗xd4 (10...♘d7!?), and now 11.♕xa8 would just transpose to the immediate capture on a8. **10...♕b6!** After 10...♗xe4 the queen escapes from a8: 11.♘c3 ♗xc2 12.♕xa7. **11.♘d2**

11...♗xd4! Eliminating ♘d2-c4 and making it a genuine rook sac. As a result the white queen remains out of play and the white king comes under fire. **12.gxf3 ♗xf2+ 13.♔d1 0-0 14.♘c4 ♕c7 15.♔e2 ♗g3 16.♖g1 ♗h2 17.♖g2 ♘d7 18.♕xf8+ ♔xf8 19.♖xh2 d5** and Gulko wrapped up efficiently (0-1, 30).

So what should White have done on move 10? Actually, there was a third possibility, which doesn't capture anything: 10.♘d2!! Activating the knight and preserving all threats. Great composure is required to find such an amazing move behind the board! Just as you will need to keep a cool head when facing the various dangers that a cornered queen brings about, no matter what material gains have preceded. ∎

MAXIMize your Tactics

with Maxim Notkin

Find the best move in the positions below

Solutions on page 95

1. White to play and win

2. White to play and win

3. White to play and win

4. White to play and win

5. Black to play and win

6. White to play and win

7. Black to play and win

8. Black to play and win

9. Black to play and win

GIBRALTAR
INTERNATIONAL CHESS FESTIVAL

CONGRATULATIONS TO OUR GIBRALTAR MASTERS 2019 WINNERS!

GIBRALTAR MASTERS 2019 — CHAMPION

GIBRALTAR MASTERS 2019 — RUNNER-UP

GIBRALTAR MASTERS 2019 — TOP FEMALE

GIBRALTAR MASTERS 2019 — SECOND PLACE FEMALE

GM Vladislav Artemiev
(Russia) 8.5/10

GM Karthikeyan Murali
(India) 8/10

GM Tan Zhongyi
(China) 7/10

GM Mariya Muzychuk
(Ukraine) 6.5/10

For more information email **chess@caletahotel.gi** or visit **www.gibchess.com**

How does he Duda?

Magnus Carlsen was the deserved and proud champion, but arguably the greatest sensation at the recent World Blitz Championship was Jan-Krzysztof Duda. The Polish grandmaster was on a roll, finishing second after an amazing winning streak. **MAXIM DLUGY** explains what makes Duda such a fantastic blitz player.

The second King Salman World Blitz Championship, held in St. Petersburg during the final days of the past year, was full of intrigue right to the wire. Magnus Carlsen upped the stakes by scoring a point more than he did the previous year to seemingly crush the event with 17/21 points, but one player was miraculously keeping up with his inexorable pace. Newcomer Jan-Krzysztof Duda also kept winning and had Magnus wondering how that was possible.

In the end, Duda finished with 16½/21, just a half point shy of the World Champion, but two points ahead of Hikaru Nakamura, who many thought would be fighting hard for first place with Magnus.

What qualities enabled this relative newcomer from Poland to compete with the best blitz players in the world? Let me endeavour to find the secret recipe that resulted in one of the most amazing blitz streaks for a non-World Champion: Duda won all his games in rounds 9-16, notching up eight straight games against strong GMs and taking out three 2800+ blitz players in the process.

Let's pick it up at the start of this prolific run, when Duda had a mere 5/8 points to his name, not a great start for someone who would only drop 1½ more points in the next 13 games.

Mikhail Demidov
Jan-Krzysztof Duda
St Petersburg World Blitz 2018 (9)
Trompowsky Attack

1.d4 ♘f6 2.♗g5 e6 3.e4 h6 4.♗xf6 ♕xf6 5.c3 g6

It is a rare game that doesn't have Jan-Krzysztof fianchetto his queen's bishop. Playing for a win, though, means playing ...g6 for many players, so here Black follows suit.

6.♗d3 ♗g7 7.♘e2 d6 8.0-0 e5
The bishop pair allows Black the luxury of chipping at the centre from all sides. Here, too, playing for an eventual ...c5 after castling and ...♕e7 was a viable alternative.

9.f4 exd4 10.cxd4 ♗g4

Duda is not shy about forcing his opponent to think about their moves as early as possible. The threat of ...♕xd4+ has been created and it's quite easy to miss.

11.♘bc3 ♕xd4+ 12.♔h1 ♗xe2 13.♕xe2

Even though has Black won a pawn, White has quite significant compensation, and Black should have thought about damage control. Instead, Duda plays to maximize his chances, trying to keep everything he has gained.

13...c6

Objectively, after 13...0-0 14.♗c4 ♘c6 15.♖ad1 ♕f6 16.f5 the position would be roughly balanced, with both sides having things to worry about.

14.e5! 0-0 15.♖ad1 ♕b6 16.e6

Black's position is not for the faint-hearted, and is in fact totally lost. The amazing quality that Duda possesses is incredible perseverance in the face of grave danger. He really has nerves of steel, as we will see in some additional examples. Let's see how he deals with this adversity.

16...♕c7

16...f5 would lose to 17.e7 ♖e8 18.♕e6+ ♔h7 19.♘e4! ♕c7 20.♘f6+ ♗xf6 21.♕f7+.

17.f5 ♗xc3

Normal play no longer helps, so Black tries to give his opponent too many options in order to confuse him. This is a monumental approach to playing blitz! This approach would not work in a regular game, in which playing a weaker move would get punished. In blitz, however, too many choices is often not a good thing.

'Duda won eight straight games against strong GMs, taking out three 2800+ rated blitz players in the process.'

With his uncompromising maximalist style, Jan-Krzysztof Duda created a sensation as he finished second in the Blitz World Championship.

18.exf7+? Not the best intermediate move. The most demoralizing sequence would be 18.fxg6 fxg6 19.♖xf8+ ♔xf8 20.♖f1+ ♔g8 21.e7.

18...♖xf7

19.fxg6?

White is losing the thread of the position. It was time to bring in the queen to aid in the attack. After 19.♕e8+ ♖f8 20.♕e6+ ♔h8 21.fxg6 ♘d7 22.♖f7 ♖xf7 23.gxf7 ♘f6 24.bxc3 ♔g7 25.♖f1 ♕xf7 26.♕xd6, White has a huge advantage, although not necessarily decisive in blitz.

19...♖e7 20.♗c4+ d5 21.♕f3

Amazingly, Black is even slightly better here, but once again Duda goes for the most risky and aggressive possibility.

21...♗g7? With the developing alternative 21...♘d7 22.♕xc3 ♘e5 23.♗e2 ♕d6 Black consolidates his position and is fine.

22.♖xd5! For now, Mikhail Demidov is up to the task. He is on track to punish Black for his risky play.

22...♔h8

23.♖f5?? A typical case of a bad move in a critical position. Now White is lost. If he had pointed his aggression towards the real weakness in Black's camp – the h6-pawn – he would have been winning. After 23.♖h5 ♘d7 24.♕h3, there is simply no defence to 25.♖xh6+.

23...♘d7 24.♗b3 ♕d6 25.h3 ♕xg6 26.♗c2 ♕e6 27.♕d3

27...♕e3!
A nice move, which shows that Black realizes that White cannot hit h7 successfully. Somehow White thinks he can.

28.♖f8+ ♗xf8 29.♕g6 ♕g5 30.♕d3 ♘e5 31.♕e4 ♕g7 32.a4 ♖d8 33.♔h2 ♖d2 34.♗b1 ♘g4+ 35.♕xg4 ♕xg4 36.hxg4 ♗g7
White resigned.

Another excellent quality that Jan-Krzysztof possesses for blitz play is the ability to exude confidence and energy, depriving his opponents of the same. In the following game against a strong young Russian grandmaster, he spurns a draw to play on in a dubious position, which immediately gets his opponent to blunder horribly and resign.

Jan-Krzysztof Duda
Grigoriy Oparin
St Petersburg World Blitz 2018 (10)
English Opening, Symmetrical Variation

1.♘f3 ♘f6 2.c4 e6 3.♘c3 c5 4.g3 b6 5.♗g2 ♗b7 6.0-0 ♗e7 7.♖e1 ♘e4

8.d4 A rare continuation, that relies on a complicated middlegame struggle rather than a safe opening initiative after 8.♘xe4 ♗xe4 9.d3.

'Another excellent quality for blitz play is his ability to exude confidence and energy.'

8...♘xc3 9.bxc3 d6 10.e4 0-0 11.d5 e5 12.a4 ♘d7
Black should activate the bishop immediately with 12...♗c8, with a good position, because now White could keep the bishop stuck on the queenside.

13.♕d3 ♗a6 14.♖f1

As we have seen in previous games, in blitz Duda looks to attack the king instead of going for queenside pressure. Here, too, he prepares the kingside assault with f4 rather than doubling rooks on the a-file and exerting pressure on the queenside.

14...♘f6 15.♘e1 g6 16.♗h6 ♗g7 17.♗xg7 ♔xg7 18.♘c2 ♕e7 19.f4 exf4 20.gxf4 ♖ae8 21.♖ae1

21...♕h4
Not surprisingly, Black's position is quite resilient, because White has many weaknesses. Black should have removed his king from the line of fire with 21...♔h8, with a good position.

22.♖e3 ♘f6 23.♖h3 ♕g4 24.♖g3 ♕h4 25.♘e3
Objectively, White is not better and should have repeated moves with 25.♖h3, but that's not Duda! Now, after 25...♗c8, Black is simply better, since White no longer has a way to oust Black's queen from h4, while his central break leads nowhere. Instead of this Black, thinking only about his own ideas, blundered horribly with:

25...♘h5?? 26.♘f5+ And Black resigned.

Jan-Krzysztof Duda
Nikita Vitiugov
St Petersburg World Blitz 2018 (12)

position after 30.♕e2

In his game against Nikita Vitiugov, Duda misplayed a nice opening to find himself in this miserable position. Let's take a look at how he extricates himself from this predicament.

30...♘g4 31.♖f1 ♘e5 32.♔g2

White cannot allow ...♕h3, so has to play this before ♘d4.

32...♘f3 33.♘d4 ♕g4?

The queen is usually a good friend to the knight in the attack on the king, but it was important to add a rook via ...♖e5-h5 or ...♖f6-h6 to break through.

34.h3 ♕g5

35.♕e3

Not the best. Amazingly, Black's active pieces are not really menacing. White had a chance to activate his queen with ♕b5, with a balanced position, e.g. 35.♕b5 ♘xd4 36.♖xd4

♖e5 37.♕xb6 ♕f5 38.♕d6 ♕f3+ 39.♔g1 ♖ef5 40.♖xd5 ♖5f6 41.♕c7 e3 42.♖d7 ♖g6 43.♖d8 ♖xg3+ 44.♕xg3 ♕xg3+ 45.fxg3 ♖xd8 46.♖e1 ♖d2, with a draw in sight.

35...♕g6 36.♘e2

Duda is true to himself. He looks for attacking moves in all positions. The tightest defence was 36.♕e2, planning to break up the pawn structure with c4. Instead, he wants to attack the d-pawn with the knight.

36...♘h4+

Bringing in the rook was still the way to break through White's position. After 36...♖e5 37.♘f4 ♛d6 Black could slowly take over all the important squares, with a decisive advantage.

37.♔h1 ♘f5

In his last blitz game in St. Petersburg, 'JKD' successfully employed a prepared opening novelty against Boris Gelfand.

38.♛f4

I hope, dear reader, that you are beginning to see the tendency. No matter what – always forward! Though this move is far weaker than the tame 38.♛d2, it forces Black to consume time looking for a way to make use of White's exposed queen position, thereby making it a good value move for blitz.

38...e3 39.f3

39...♘d6?

Here is the result of White's pushy play. Black misses the transposition to a favourable endgame with 39...♘xg3+ 40.♛xg3 ♛xg3 41.♘xg3 e2 42.♘xe2 ♖xe2 43.♖xd5? ♖xb2. Even if White played 43.♖d4, Black would retain a sizeable advantage without any risk.

40.♛d4 ♘f5

The not so obvious 40...♛c2 would leave Black better after 41.♛xd5+

♘f7, but that's already not a blitz level move.

41.♛xd5+ ♔h8 42.g4

42...♛h6?

After this move, Duda's position is finally better. 42...♘h4 was necessary to preserve the balance.

43.♔h2 ♘h4 44.f4 ♛f6 45.♖d4 ♘g6

46.♛f3

It's logical to try and consolidate in a pawn-up position, though in a tournament game the sequence 46.♖xa4 ♖d8 47.♛b5! ♖d2 48.♖e4! would be significantly more decisive.

46...♛e7 47.♖fd1 a3 48.b3 ♛c7 49.♔g1 ♘e5 50.♛g2 ♘g6

51.f5

Most strong players would continue consolidating with moves like 51.♛g3 or even 51.♖e4!, but not Duda. For him, blitz is moving forward even if the move is not objectively best.

51...♘e5

If Black had been Duda, he might have played actively with 51...♘h4! 52.♛h1 g6! 53.♖d7 ♖d8!!, with equal chances.

52.♛g3?! Once again, some important squares were lacking protection. After 52.♖f1, controlling f3, White's advantage would be nearly decisive.

52...♕c6 Here Black needed to undermine White's most advanced pawn with 52...g6, with good counterplay.

53.♖f1 Now the best move was 53.♖d5!, forcing Black's knight back to f7, but it looks as if Duda wanted to start preparing a kingside assault with his pawns instead.

53...h6?
Once again, 53...g6 would have given Black good counterplay, but Vitiugov simply misses this entire idea.
54.♔h2 b5 55.h4

55...h5? Amazingly, even now 55...g6 still equalizes! After 55...g6 56.♖df4 g5! 57.hxg5 hxg5 58.♖d4 ♔g7 White has to start defending, and if White doesn't capture on g5, Black takes on h4, eyeing f3 with his knight, with a draw.
56.gxh5 ♕h6 57.♕g5 ♔h7 58.♔h3 ♖f6 59.♕xh6+
Instead, 59.♖e4! was immediately

decisive, since the queen can't go anywhere. The pin is crushing.
59...♔xh6 60.♖e4 ♖ff8 61.♖xe3 ♘d7 62.♖xe8 ♖xe8 63.♘g3?
A serious mistake. It was time to start collecting the pawns on the queenside with 63.♘d4, as 63...♖e3+ would be met by 64.♖f3.

63...♖e3! Now the position is suddenly equal! **64.c4 bxc4 65.bxc4 ♘f6 66.♔g2 ♖c3 67.♖f2 ♖xc4 68.♖e2 ♘xh5 69.♖e8**

69...♘f4+ Incredible how many blunders players make against Duda! Black has an elementary draw with 69...♖xh4 or 69...♖c2+, and yet decides to play for his own mate. There is only one reasonable explanation: When your opponent presses you for over 60 moves in blitz, you get tired, lose focus and blunder. Let's see the end of this dramatic game:
70.♔f3 g6 71.f6 ♘d5 72.♖h8
Mate.

'Duda looks for the most aggressive move in blitz from any position, making him a very difficult player to play.'

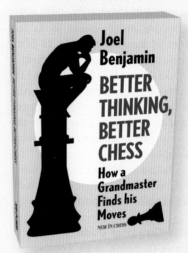

When I teach chess, I use a phrase: 'retreat as little as possible', meaning that when you are attacked, you should actually try to move the piece up the board whenever possible, towards your opponent. If you must go back, go back the least possible number of squares. This will ensure that you will also look for the most aggressive move. Duda looks for the most aggressive move in blitz from any position, making him a very difficult player to play. While he gives you chances to get a great position, he is also looking to crush you at all times, and after a while the pressure proves too much for most of his opponents.

Let's take a look at a couple of more atypical-looking crushes by Duda against seasoned opposition.

Jan-Krzysztof Duda
Boris Gelfand
St Petersburg World Blitz 2018 (21)
Trompowsky Attack

1.d4 ♘f6 2.♗g5 d5 3.♗xf6 gxf6 4.c4 dxc4 5.e3 c5 6.d5 b5 7.a4 ♗b7 8.axb5 ♕xd5 9.♕xd5 ♗xd5 10.♘c3 ♗b7 11.♗e2!

Considering how fast Jan-Krzysztof played this move, it was clearly a prepared novelty. Previously, 11.f3 was played in one game, which Black managed to win.

11...♘d7?!

Boris should have taken the pawn. After 11...♗xg2 12.♗f3 ♗xf3 13.♘xf3 ♘d7 14.♔e2 ♘b6 15.♖a6 ♗g7 16.♖ha1 0-0 17.♖xa7 ♖xa7 18.♖xa7 f5! Black has excellent

chances to equalize, although it is clear that this would not be obvious to someone not having analysed the position before.

12.♗f3 ♗xf3 13.♘xf3

13...e6

Here, too, the plan with ...♘b6, ...♗g7 and ...0-0 was the best defensive plan for Black, although White would be much better. Now White demolishes the queenside.

14.♘d2

14...f5?

Characteristically, Boris is looking for active play, but this move simply fails to defend against White's threats. After the best defence 14...♘b6 15.♖a6 ♗d6 16.♔d1! (White's c3-pawn needs protection if Black plays ...♗e5xc3, so this is the strongest continuation) 16...0-0 17.♔c2 ♗e5 18.♖ha1 ♖fb8 19.♖xa7 ♖xa7 20.♖xa7 ♗xh2 21.♘de4, White would still be on the way to scoring a point, but finding the prophylactic manoeuvre ♔d1-c2 is far from obvious.

15.♘xc4 ♗g7 16.b6 ♔e7 17.b7 ♖ab8 18.♖xa7 ♘e5 19.♘a5 ♖hd8 20.♔e2 ♔d7 21.♖d1+ ♔c7

22.♘b5+ ♔b6 23.♖xd8 ♖xd8 24.♖a8

Black resigned.

As you can see, developing your own opening ideas in off-beat variations like the Trompowsky can go a long way towards winning points in blitz!

Jan-Krzysztof Duda
Levon Aronian
St Petersburg World Blitz 2018 (15)

position after 25.♖e2

To make my point, in this position against Levon Aronian, Duda achieved a significant advantage with a nicely placed knight on c5. Instead of retreating from the pin with 25...♕c7, Aronian decided to resolve the issue by taking out the knight on the spot and played **25...♘xc5??** There followed **26.dxc5** and he resigned.

Now what would make a super-GM fall apart like that in a blitz game? Clearly the confidence, the speed and the ongoing pressure by Jan-Krzysztof Duda that comes with it, leaves its mark on even the best.

So, play actively, aggressively and quickly and you too shall do well in blitz!! ∎

MAXIMize your Tactics Solutions

1. Menna-Hoffman
Rio de Janeiro 2018

2. Kociscak-Tazbir
Czech Republic 2018

3. Lahaye-Jedlicka
Groningen 2018

29.♖xc5! ♕xc5 30.♗d4! The bishop is immune due to 31.♕e8 mate. 30...♕e7 31.♗xa7 leaves White with an extra piece. Black resigned.

Black has pinned his hopes on ...♖c8 but... **35.♖xf8+! ♔xf8 36.♗xd6+!** Black resigned as after 36....♖xd6 37.♕a8+ he is checkmated.

55.♕f8+ ♔g6 56.♗xf5+! 56...♗xf5 57.♕e8+ Black resigned in view of 57...♔h6 58.♗f8+; 57...♔g7 58.♗e5+; or 57...♔f6 58.♕h8+!.

4. Napoli-Suarez
Elgoibar 2018

5. Bocharov-Pershin
St. Petersburg 2018

6. Solomon-Papin
Melbourne 2018

14.♗xf7+! ♔xf7 If 14...♕xf7 15.e6 ♕f8 (15...♕xe6 16.♖e4) 16.exd7+ ♗xd7 17.♕g6+ ♔d8 18.♖d2 and 19.♖hd1. **15.♖f4+ ♘f6 16.e6+!** Black loses the queen after 16...♗xe6 17.♘e5+, so he resigned.

33...♖xf3! 34.♖g6!? 34.♔xf3 ♕f7+ loses the queen by a rook check. **34...♖xf2+!** 34...♖ff6 35.♗xf6 ♕f7 36.♕c2! would be more or less equal. **35.♔e1 ♖ff6! 36.♗xf6 ♕f7** White resigned.

36.e5! ♖g8 36...dxe5 37.♖xd8; 36...fxe5 37.♖f4! ♖f8 38.♗h5. **37.exf6+ ♔d7 38.♖xd6+ ♔c7 39.♖d7+ ♔b8 40.♖xf7 ♕b3** 40...♖xg7+ 41.fxg7 and ♖dd7. **41.♖xb7+** (41.♖dd7!) and the ending was won.

7. Praggnanandhaa-Anand
Kolkata blitz 2018

8. Repka-Sonis
Montebelluna 2018

9. Le Quang Liem-Bersamina
Makati 2018

21...♗xe4! 22.fxe4 After 22.♗d1 ♕xa3+ 23.♔d2 ♗xf3 Black's attack rages on. **22...♕a1+ 23.♔d2 ♘xe4+ 24.♔e3 ♕c3+!** 25.♗d3 If 25.♔xe4 d5+! 26.♔xd5 ♖d8+ and mate. **25...♕d2+ 26.♔xe4 ♕xh6** and Black went on to win.

Instead of 24...♕d4+ 25.♘c4 Black could win with **24...♖xa5+! 25.♔xa5** (25.♕xa5 b5+ 26.♔b4 ♕d2+) **25...♕a3+ 26.♗a4 ♖d8! 27.♘xc6 ♕d5+ 28.♖b5 b6+ 29.♔a6 ♕xa4+ 30.♖a5 ♕c4+! 31.♔xa7 ♖d7+** and mate.

34...h3! 35.♖xc7 35.gxh3 ♘xh3+ 36.♔g2 ♕f4; or 35.g3 h2+! 36.♘xh2 ♖xh2! with ...♗f3 and mate. **35...hxg2 36.♘h2 ♗f3!** To 37.♗f5/♕e6, covering h3, Black replies 37...♗xc7, when 38...♘e2+ and ...♗xh2 mate is unavoidable. White resigned.

Truly inexhaustible

So many fascinating books are written about so many different subjects within chess, concludes our reviewer **MATTHEW SADLER**. Two recent ones he recommends with '5 shining stars': a majestic biography of German master *Kurt Richter* and Jan Timman's unputdownable *The Longest Game* on the five epic matches Karpov and Kasparov contested.

Living in England at the current time is living with an obsession: Brexit (Britain's decision to leave the European Union). A favourite game with British citizens is to try to spend a whole day without hearing the dreaded word. I thought I might be on a winner when I visited our Dutch office last week, only to be greeted with 'Hey, Mr Brexit!'. Even a talk on AlphaZero in London to a mixture of AI and chess enthusiasts wasn't safe territory. One of the questions – more a plea actually – was whether AlphaZero might be able to replace our politicians and help us find a path through this complicated mess! The question was greeted with a huge cheer and a round of applause!

At the same talk, the mother of a very keen young chess player asked whether it was worth her son spending any effort on chess when computers were stronger than humans. It's a very sensible question, but I would have loved to have been able to answer by pointing to a pile of chess books – like the books I've been reviewing this month – to say: 'this is why chess is worth the effort!'. So many fascinating books are written about so many different subjects within chess: chess truly feels inexhaustible!

■ ■ ■

We start with a wonderful biography of the German master *Kurt Richter* by Alan McGowan (McFarland & Company). The secret of a great biography is not only to describe the subject but also the era in which he lived. Genna Sosonko is a master at this in his biographies of the great Russian players such as Bronstein, Kortchnoi and Smyslov, evocatively conveying the somewhat sinister atmosphere of Soviet Russia. This book does the same for the German chess scene before and after World War II, with a wealth of detail, tournament cross tables and photos. I was more and more intrigued with every page I read. For example, who was this German master Ludwig Rödl, who at the age of 24 tied for first with Bogoljubow – then at the peak of his powers – in the German Championship of 1931? (In fact, Rödl was a point clear before the last round but lost to Ahues and then lost the playoff.) In 1932 he came second to Stoltz in a strong tournament at Swinemünde and then second to Bogoljubow at the German Championship of 1933 in Bad Pyrmont. A strong player, yet totally unknown to me!

But perhaps I should get back to describing the book! It's a huge volume of 368 very large pages, beautifully hardbound. The book covers Richter's chess life from his first tentative steps in 1919 (aged 19) to his final game in 1962. He died on 29th December 1969.

Richter was both a successful player and a chess journalist, editing three German chess periodicals and writing numerous articles in other publications. He was famous during his career for his uncompromising attacking style ('... with Richter it rages' was Tartakower's famous comment) and original aggressive openings, in particular 1.d4 d5 2.♘c3 ♘f6 3.♗g5 which he played all his life as White. Richter's career is divided into nine chapters and the book is rounded off with four appendices: additional games, a complete tournament record and two summaries of Richter's contribution to opening theory with White and with Black. There are many interesting passages of text – for example when McGowan considers Richter's chess activities during and after World War II – but it would be remiss to carry on any longer without talking about the wonderful games that Richter played. What an uncompromising player and what a legacy of attacking games! Firstly, there are the flights of fancy in the opening. How about this...

Kurt Richter
Ludwig Rellstab
Munich 1942
King's Indian Defence,
Accelerated Averbakh System

1.d4 ♘f6 2.♗g5 g6 3.c4 ♗g7 4.♘c3 d6 5.e4 ♘bd7 6.f4 0-0 7.g4

1-0, 39.

He played a variety of enterprising openings with Black, such as the Fajarowicz (1.d4 ♘f6 2.c4 e5 3.dxe5 ♘e4), the Polish Defence (1.d4 b5) and the Scandinavian (1.e4 d5 2.exd5 ♘f6), when he even met 3.c4 with 3...b5! Or even on one occasion, the 'Basman-iac' 1...g5!

Paul Michel
Kurt Richter
Bad Oeynhausen 1938
Reversed Grob

1.e4 g5 2.d4 h6 3.f4 ♗g7 4.c3 gxf4 5.♗xf4 c5 6.dxc5 b6 7.♕g4 ♔f8 8.♕g3 ♘a6 9.cxb6 ♕xb6

½-½, 29.

...which I think is a position that Michael would feel extremely at home in! However, I would like to show you some of his games against the French Defence which he reached either directly via 1.e4 e6 or via a transposition when starting with 1.d4 d5 2.♘c3 ♘f6 3.♗g5 e6 4.e4. In particular, his play against the Classical 4...♗e7 led to some deeply impressive and beautiful games.

Kurt Richter
Erwin Kipke
Berlin 1934
French Defence,
Anderssen-Richter Variation

The following casual game was entertainingly annotated by Richter as a conversation with an imaginary Dr. Zabel – a method he used many times in his writings.

1.e4 e6 2.d4 d5 3.♘c3 ♘f6 4.♗g5 ♗e7 5.♗xf6 This and particularly the follow-up with 6.e5 and 7.♕g4 was Richter's patent.

Strangely enough, a match in 1894 between Showalter and Albin was virtually a theme match for the position after 7.♕g4: it occurred no less than 8 times(!), with Albin scoring three wins and two losses as Black.

5...♗xf6 6.e5 ♗e7 7.♕g4 0-0 8.♗d3 8.0-0-0 was the move order Richter switched to later, to avoid the possibility of 8.♗d3 f5 9.♕h3 c5 10.dxc5 ♕a5, when the threat of 11...d4 will prevent White from castling queenside easily (11.0-0-0 d4 will win the a2-pawn).

8...f5 9.♕h3 c5 10.dxc5 ♘c6 10...♘d7 11.f4 ♘xc5 12.0-0-0 b5 was Albin's successful choice in two games (he also played one game preparing the advance first with

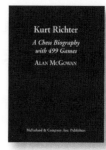

Kurt Richter
Alan McGowan
McFarland, 2018
★★★★★

12...♗d7 before following up later with ...b5) and it was the continuation that Richter most struggled against: he lost three games in this line over the years. After 13.♘f3 (varying from Showalter's 13.♘ce2, but not with great success) 13...b4 14.♘e2 ♘xd3+ 15.♖xd3 (15.cxd3 b3 is nasty) 15...♗a6 16.♖d2 ♗xe2 17.♖xe2, my engine recommends a more direct implementation of Black's queenside attack with 17...a5 followed by ...♕b6, ...a4 and a rook to the c-file. White is in big trouble. In the game, Black also won in 67 moves – Richter-Koch, Berlin 1951. However, let's leave such

'The secret of a great biography is not only to describe the subject but also the era in which he lived.'

finesses behind and see the positive aspects of Richter's line!

11.f4 ♗xc5 11...♕a5 12.0-0-0 d4 13.♘b1 ♕xa2 14.g4

is an encapsulation of the full subtlety of Richter's plan: open the g-file and then mate! 14...b6 15.gxf5 exf5 16.♘e2 bxc5 17.♖hg1 ♕d5 18.♖g3

'What an uncompromising player and what a legacy of attacking games!'

c4 19.♖dg1 ♖f7 20.♕h6 g5 21.♗xc4 ♕xc4 22.♖xg5+ ♔xg5 23.♕xg5+ ♔f8 24.♕h6+ (24...♔e8 25.♖g8+ ♔d7 26.♕d6 mate, easy to miss) 1-0, Richter-Wächter, Swinemünde 1936.
12.♘ge2 Slightly unexpected development, but 12.♘f3 followed by 0-0-0 would give Black the resource of ...♗e3+xf4.
12...a6 13.0-0-0 b5 14.g4 b4 15.gxf5

A motif that you see frequently in Richter's games in these lines.
15...exf5 15...bxc3 16.f6 cxb2+ 17.♔b1 'and this attacking position seemed to me to be worth the piece.' After an initial burst of scepticism, my engine pulls back to a 0.00 evaluation, after seeing some more moves on the board: 17...g6 18.♕g3 followed by h4-h5 is easy play for White and Black isn't set up to exploit the weakened white queenside yet.
16.♘a4 ♕a5 16...♗a7 was better according to Richter, keeping the white rooks away from the g-file for now.
17.♘xc5 ♕xc5 18.♖hg1 ♔h8
19.♘g3 Bringing a knight into play close to the opponent's king, having first opened a file on the kingside. It's probably due to my current obsession, but I can't help thinking of AlphaZero's play!
19...♘d4 20.♔b1 a5 21.♘h5 ♖a7 22.♖g6

A great way of doubling rooks on the g-file, though my engine is now not impressed with White's chances!
22...a4 22...hxg6 23.♘f6 mate.
23.♖dg1 b3 24.♖xg7 bxc2+ 25.♔c1 ♘b3+
25...a3 is recommended by Richter and is apparently completely winning for Black! 26.♖xa7 ♕xa7 27.♕g3 ♗e6. The text also looks pretty good for Black.
26.axb3 axb3 How does White stop ...♖a1, as 27.♖xa7 hits on 27...♕xg1+ ?

27.♗a6 What a move! **27...♗xa6** 27...♖xa6 28.♖xh7+ ♔xh7 29.♘f6 mate; 27...♕a5 28.♖xa7 ♕a1+ 29.♔d2 ♕xg1 30.♖xh7+. **28.♕g3** The bishop on a6 blocks the a-file now, so the threat of 29.♖g8+ is decisive (28...♕c8 29.♖xa7). 1-0

A treasure trove of games and a wonderful overview of the German chess scene of this period! 5 shining stars!

■ ■ ■

When I saw that Jan Timman was releasing a book on the five Kasparov-Karpov matches – *The Longest Game* (New In Chess) – I was somewhat dubious. It was funny to read the foreword and hear that Jan had also had his doubts in the beginning – in fact the same doubts that I had! After all, much had been written about the matches, including several books by Kasparov himself! What could there be to add to that? As Jan puts it: 'Kasparov's stories are based on his own viewpoints. There was enough room for other stories and anecdotes. In his analyses, Kasparov often loses his way in a forest of variations. A slightly lighter form of annotations might make the games more accessible (...) And there was yet another consideration: since the appearance of Kasparov's books, computers had become much stronger. Part of his analyses would not hold out against the new cybernetic findings (...) With 50 annotated games and 17 fragments, I have tried to bring these five matches back to life. Thus, I have created a reader as well as an instruction book, since there is a lot to be learned from the games of this epic battle.'

The idea of turning these great matches into a book both entertaining and instructive really appealed to me. I think there is also a further point: reflecting on these matches after a period of many years from a chess world that has changed so much (can you imagine: no computers, no databases!) is a useful and interesting exercise in itself – doubly so from a great player who has experienced all of these events himself at the highest level.

So, I thought, let's read it then... and I found it hard to put down! There is something extremely satisfying about reading about events that you know well, and then discovering that you've forgotten or never noticed some important details! I had this feeling constantly while playing through the games or reading the accompanying story behind those great matches.

Perhaps the most astonishing fact mentioned by Timman is that there was a ban on writing down variations inside the Kasparov camp! I understand the reasons, but it still shocked me: I can't imagine living with the risk of losing key variations by forgetting them! However, interesting though all the politics and background stories are, it's the quality of the games that still astounds. Pre-computer age, but these players played at such a level! One game I particularly liked was the 22nd match game from the 1985 match in Moscow. Somehow it had completely escaped my attention all these years, but it's a beautifully thematic exploitation of a kingside pawn majority, and a few extracts from the notes gives you an idea of how Timman annotates these games.

**The Longest Game
Jan Timman
New In Chess, 2018**
★★★★★

**Anatoly Karpov
Garry Kasparov**
Moscow KK2 1985 (22)
Queen's Gambit Declined,
Charousek Variation

**1.d4 d5 2.c4 e6 3.♘c3 ♗e7
4.cxd5 exd5 5.♗f4 ♘f6 6.e3 0-0
7.♘f3 ♗f5 8.h3 c6 9.g4 ♗g6
10.♘e5 ♘fd7 11.♘xg6 fxg6
12.♗g2 ♘b6 13.0-0 ♔h8**

14.♘e2
The most direct plan would have been the one introduced by 14.♗h2, with the intention of pushing the e-pawn. The play can then develop as follows: 14.♗h2 ♗d6 15.♗xd6 ♕xd6 16.e4 ♘a6 (16...dxe4, releasing the tension, has its downsides: after 17.♘xe4, White brings his knight to c5, the

e6-square is a serious weakness in the black camp) 17.exd5 (17.e5 doesn't yield anything after 17...♕b4, the white d-pawn becomes weak) 17...♘xd5 18.♘xd5 cxd5 19.♕b3 ♘c7 20.♖ac1, and White has pressure on the enemy position.

'The quality of the games still astounds.'

Nevertheless, it is understandable that Karpov didn't want to let it come to this. In this type of open game, the drawing tendencies are fairly large. Therefore he opts for a more circumspect plan, maintaining the half-closed character of the position.
14...g5 15.♗g3 ♗d6 16.♕d3 ♘a6 17.b3 ♕e7 18.♗xd6 ♕xd6 19.f4 gxf4 20.exf4 ♖ae8 21.f5 ♘c7 22.♖f2 ♘d7 23.g5

White further expands his majority undisturbed, ceding the e-file to his opponent.
23...♕e7 For the time being, White has no direct threats, but his pawn front constitutes a latent danger for Black, in the middlegame as well as in the endgame.

24.h4 ♕e3 A wise decision. Black aims for the exchange of queens to give his control of the e-file a permanent character.
25.♖d1 ♘b5 26.♕xe3 This is not very accurate, since now the black rook will be very active on e3. 26.♗h3 looked stronger, with the intention of bringing the knight to f4.
26...♖xe3 27.♔h2 ♘b6 28.♘g3 ♘c8 This little move must have been underestimated by Karpov. The knight is on its way to d6, after which White runs the risk that his position comes under pressure.
29.♘f1 Otherwise White cannot make any good progress. First he has to drive the rook from its dominating position.
29...♖e7 The first inaccuracy. There was nothing against 29...♖c3, to keep the rook as active as possible. White then has to maintain the equilibrium. 30.♘g3 is met by 30...♘cd6 after which Black can look to the future with confidence.
30.♖d3 A small success. White controls the position again.
30...♘cd6 31.♘g3 ♘e4 The second inaccuracy. This results in a loss of positional trumps: his control of the e-file and the strong knight on d6.
32.♗xe4 dxe4 33.♖e3 ♘xd4 34.♔h3

Black has temporarily won a pawn, but with the text move, Karpov demonstrates that he has the advantage. The king will go to g4, supporting the pawn front. Winning back the e-pawn is just a question of time.

34...♖e5 35.♔g4 h5+ The third inaccuracy, which leads to a lost position. Kasparov was in time-trouble and fell prey to his old weakness: making random pawn moves. He should have settled for passive defence with 35...♖fe8.
36.♔xh5 ♘xf5 37.♖xf5 ♖fxf5 38.♘xf5 ♖xf5 39.♖xe4 The rook ending is hopeless for Black. He cannot prevent the white rook from invading on e7, with devastation.
39...♔h7 40.♖e7 b5 41.♖xa7 b4 42.♔g4 1-0.

I really like these annotations. Clear and concise, pointing out all the key moments in the game as well as some excellent positional instruction. A really good book – 5 stars!

■ ■ ■

I mentioned Genna Sosonko before in this review, so you won't be too surprised to learn that I also enjoyed his *Smyslov on the Couch* (Elk and Ruby) greatly. It's a book that once again captures the personality of a great player, the era in which he lived and – just as poignantly as with Bronstein – the struggle of growing old, to which the whole of the third section ('The Final Years') is dedicated. Smyslov and his wife grew old together, he losing his sight but still composing studies. They were rich, but unsure who to trust while needing help, and so their world shrank to looking after the beautiful cat Belka that had adopted them.

'Constant griping about ubiquitous theft and deception became the main focus of his monologues. It's very possible there were grounds for that, although Mikhail Beilin, his second, co-author and neighbour who'd known the seventh world champion in his prime, recalled: "The Smyslovs feared that someone would break into their home, deceive them or steal from them even back then, but this anxiety grew much more severe during the last years of their lives.

"Actually, they were impoverished

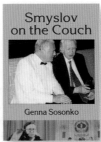

Smyslov on the Couch
Genna Sosonko
Elk and Ruby, 2018
★★★★☆

Understanding before Moving Part 1: Ruy Lopez and Italian Structures
Herman Grooten
Thinkers Publishing, 2018
★★★☆☆

millionaires. This happens more often than you would think: you may have read about someone discovering that a man dying in utter destitution actually had a fat sum – like thousands of dollars if not more – in his bank account or under his mattress, but the Smyslovs were a completely different case. You didn't have to be a financial whiz to realise that their apartment in central Moscow, garage and dacha

'Constant griping about ubiquitous theft and deception became the main focus of Smyslov's monologues.'

with its sizeable land plot in Razdory were worth a few million dollars, but they were too haunted by thoughts that they would be cheated, deceived or even killed to take any steps to improve their financial situation. So they didn't have the cash to cover their daily expenses, especially during their last few years when they truly needed help. Therefore those who saw them, a bit dishevelled-looking, ungroomed and not always speaking coherently, at their near dilapidated dacha, spoke about the shocking impression they made."'

Again, a short but really interesting book about Sosonko's interaction with a great of chess history. Recommended!

■ ■ ■

We round off with the start of what could become an interesting series of books for the club player: *Understanding before moving: Part I. Ruy Lopez – Italian Structures* by Herman Grooten (Thinkers Publishing). This series of books aims to give club players an insight into the strategical goals of the opening, provide an overview of the main variations and teach readers how to study, learn and understand the opening phase in general. This book covers the most frequent lines of the Ruy Lopez and Italian Game (including the Two Knights), ending with twelve exercises for the reader to test his acquired knowledge.

It's a lovely idea, and I could imagine that I would have been very keen on such a book as a junior. My only criticism is that Grooten spreads his net in this book a little too widely. I had assumed that – just like the ChessBase DVD by Tiviakov *Attacking with the Italian Game and Ruy Lopez* – the book would focus on a small number of typical structures such as the d3-e4 structures with the light-squared bishop outside the pawn chain, and examine the rich and varied plans available to both sides from there. Grooten instead covers all manner of systems such as the Marshall, the Italian Two Knights and the Zaitsev System, which have little in common with each other. I wonder whether the variety of material covered might be confusing for the reader, and whether a more restricted scope might have achieved more. However, there are plenty of interesting and worthwhile tips so it's definitely a book worth buying as part of a general opening study of king's pawn openings. ■

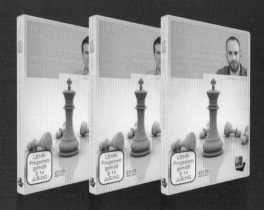

Jan Timman

Waiting for a mistake

The way Magnus Carlsen clinched victory at the Tata Steel tournament may not be to everyone's taste, but endgame lover **JAN TIMMAN** found the World Champion's strategy of patience and persistence fascinating. Until the last round, that is.

Magnus Carlsen was in an excellent mood on the eve of the Tata Steel tournament. He was eager to play a tournament again after his nerve-wracking match against Caruana. I know from experience that matches in the World Championship cycle are a serious assault on your system: the never-ending tension before and during the match, the ceaseless opening preparation in which accuracy is the key word, and the same opponent, day in, day out. After all this it's a relief to play a tournament again. You can wander around and watch other games, the pressure of opening preparation is less onerous and you don't have a sword of Damocles hovering above your head when a game goes wrong.

Yet Carlsen found it hard to get going. After three draws he seemed to have made a principled decision: accepting his relative lack of form, he would concentrate on winning the endgames. His intended motto may have gone something like this:

no more heavy-duty opening preparation, go for equal positions and wait for your opponent to make a mistake. It's quite possible, of course, that his line of thought was less rational and that he just played for what he was worth. In that case, this is only my interpretation of his play.

In Round 3, we got a taste of what he could do in the endgame: against Vidit he tried for almost 100 moves to win a four vs three rook ending. The Indian grandmaster didn't budge, though. Many chess fans will be disappointed and lose interest when they see such a game, but I find it fascinating. I love the endgame and admire extreme over-the-board fanaticism. I love watching someone trying to get the most out of almost nothing.

Carlsen failed against Vidit, but that endgame was not too difficult to defend. Three rounds later, however, things got very interesting.

'I love the endgame and admire extreme over-the-board fanaticism.'

Magnus Carlsen
Shakhriyar Mamedyarov
Wijk aan Zee 2019 (6)

position after 27.♘b3

In a Queen's Gambit Accepted, Carlsen had released the central tension at an early stage, and after a queen swap this non-descript position had arisen. In the diagrammed position, accurate play by Black is still required to equalize, however.
27... ♗f6
Black would have been better off trying to swap the other bishops with 27...♘5b6, after which White has no more advantage worth talking about.
28. ♗xf6 ♔xf6 29.♘bc5
Transferring the other knight to c5 would have been more accurate. After 29.♘dc5 ♘xc5 30.♘xc5, White is slightly better.

29...♘5b6!
This is the difference. Black is not forced to swap on c5.
30. ♗e2 ♘c4 31.a4 ♘db6

With 31...♘xc5 32.♘xc5 ♗d5, Black could have equalized relatively simply, but Mamedyarov, true to form, is looking for complications.

32.a5 ♘d5 33.♘xa6

33...♘dxe3+ This was his idea. Black gets a rook and pawn against two minor pieces and takes the initiative.

34.fxe3 ♘xe3+ 35.♔g1 ♘xd1 36.♖xd1 ♖c2

36...♖c3 was also possible. After 37.♘ac5 e5 38.♖f1 e4 39.♘f2 ♔e5 40.♗xb5 ♖d2 the position is equal.

37.♗f3 ♗e4 Again, Black had a playable alternative: after 37...♗xf3 38.gxf3 ♖d4 39.♘ac5 ♖h4 40.♖e1 ♖xh3 41.♖xe6+ ♔g7 42.♖e7+ ♔f6, the game would have been drawn by force.

38.♘ac5 ♗xd3

'After three rounds, Magnus Carlsen seemed to have made a principled decision, accepting his relative lack of form, he would concentrate on winning the endgames.'

39.♖xd3 With 39.♘xd3 White could have set a trap: after 39...e5 40.♖f1, Black must not capture on d3 in view of 41.♗e4. Correct is 40...♖d4 41.♘f2 ♔g7, again with an equal position.

39...♖xd3 40.♘xd3 e5 41.♗b7 e4 42.♘c5 ♔e5 43.a6 ♖a2 44.♗c6

44...h5? Was Mamedyarov playing to win? With 44...♔d4 45.♗xb5 e3, he could have maintained the balance. White's pawns are unable to advance.

45.♗xb5 g4

Black seems to want to steer the white king into a mating net, but this plan is doomed to fail.

It was too late for 45...♔d4 now, incidentally, because White can shield the a-file with 46.♘a4 or 46.♗a4, after which the way for the a-pawn is clear.

46.hxg4 hxg4 47.♗c4

The simple refutation of Black's plan.

47...♖a1+ 48.♔h2 f4 49.b5 f3 50.b6 ♔f4 51.♘xe4 1-0.

Especially psychologically, this was a strong game. Mamedyarov was in poor form, and by playing mainly quiet and unambitious chess Carlsen managed to draw him out.

Carlsen was hardly ever in danger throughout the tournament. Only in his game against Fedoseev did he have to fight hard for a draw.

Vladimir Fedoseev
Magnus Carlsen
Wijk aan Zee 2019 (7)

position after 22.♖c2

Black has lost a pawn and will have to go all out to get a draw.

22...♖ac8

The best choice. After 22...♘xb2 23.♘xc4 ♖ac8 24.♖xb2 ♖xc4 25.♖b7, White has good winning chances.

23.♗g5 After 23.♖d1, Black had prepared 23...♗xb2 24.♘xc4 ♗f6, gaining a tempo by attacking the h-pawn.

23...♖e8 24.♘xc4 h6 25.♗f4 ♘b4 26.♖cc1

26...♘xa2 Again the best defence. After 26...♘d3 27.♖cd1 ♘xf4 28.♘d6 ♘e2+ 29.♔h1 ♖ed8 30.♘xc8 ♖xc8 31.♖d2, White would have realistic winning chances.

27.♖a1 ♖xc4 28.♖xa2 ♗e5

Carlsen liquidates to a double rook ending that will end up in a four vs three situation on the kingside.

29.b3 ♖b4 30.♗xe5 ♖xe5 31.♖xa6 ♖xb3 32.♖d1 ♖b4 33.♖d7 ♔g7 34.♖aa7 ♖f5 35.f3

35...♖b2!

A strong little move that keeps the king in its place.

36.e4 ♖f4 37.e5 ♖e2 38.♖e7 ♖f5

Black temporarily sacrifices a second pawn in order to get a theoretical endgame.

39.e6 ♔f8 40.♖xf7+ ♖xf7 41.♖xf7+ ♔g8 42.♖e7 ♔f8

43.♖f7+ ♔g8 44.h5 gxh5 45.♖f5 ♖xe6 46.♖xh5 ♔g7 47.♔f2 ♖a6 48.g4 ♖a2+ 49.♔g3 ♖a3 50.♖d5 ♔f6 51.♔f4 ♖a4+ 52.♔e3 ♖a1 53.f4 ♖g1 54.♖d6+ ♔g7 55.♔f3 ♖e1 56.♖b6 ♖g1 57.♖e6 ♖a1 58.♔e4 ♖a4+ 59.♔f5 ♖a5+ 60.♖e5 ♖a7 61.♖d5 ♖f7+ 62.♔e4 ♖e7+ 63.♔d4 ♖e1 64.♖d7+ ♔f6 65.♖d6+ ♔g7 66.♔d5 ♖g1 67.♔e6 ♖xg4 68.♖d7+ ♔g8 69.f5 ♖f4 70.♔f6 ♖f1 71.♖d8+ ♔h7 72.♖d7+ ♔g8 73.♖d8+ ♔h7 74.♖d7+

Draw. As he pointed out at the final press conference, Carlsen was very satisfied with his well-calculated defence in this endgame.

After eight rounds, Carlsen and Anand shared the lead with 5.5 points. In Round 9, they met each other in Leiden. Again, Carlsen took it easy, winning far into a long endgame because Anand got tired.

Magnus Carlsen
Vishy Anand
Wijk aan Zee 2019 (10)

position after 24...♖xd8

White has not achieved much, but he has something to play for.

25.f5 exf5

It was hard to see, but 25...♖d5 was the best defence. After 26.f6+ gxf6 27.♘xf6 ♖xe5 28.♘xh7 b5, White cannot make progress, despite his two connected passed pawns.

26.gxf5 ♖f8 27.f6+ Now White is better, especially because he has square g5 for his knight.

27...gxf6 28.exf6+ ♔f7 29.♖f4

♘g6 30.♘g5+ ♔e8 31.♖f1 h6 32.♘e6 ♖f7 33.♖d1

The best plan. White gives up his strong passed pawn in exchange for two black queenside pawns.

33...♖xf6 34.♘xc7+ ♔f8 35.♘xa6 ♘f4 36.h4 ♘g6 37.♖h1 ♖f7

38.h5

Inaccurate; this moves renders the h-pawn more vulnerable. With 38.a4, White could have kept his winning chances alive.

38...♘f4 39.a4 ♔e7 40.♘c7 ♔f6 41.♘b5 ♔g5 42.♘d6 ♖e6 43.♔b2 ♖e6 44.♘f7+ ♔f5 45.♖d1 ♔g4 46.♔c3 ♔xh5 47.♖h1+ ♔g6 48.♘xh6 ♖e4 49.♔b2 ♖e2 50.♘g4

'Now, as in his final match game against Caruana, Carlsen didn't seem to care.'

50...♘d3+

Impatience. Black is aiming for a rook swap, believing that the resulting knight ending will be drawn. But 50...♔f5 was stronger, because the white knight would be dominated, and Black wouldn't even be worse.

51.♔c3 ♘b4 52.♖h2 ♖xh2 53.♘xh2 ♔f5 54.♘f3 ♔e4 55.♘e1 ♔d5 56.♘d3 ♘c6 57.♘f4+ ♔d6 58.♔c4 ♘a7 59.♘d5 ♔c6 60.♘e7+ ♔d6 61.♘f5+ ♔c6 62.♔d3 ♔c7 63.♔e4 ♘c6 64.♘e3 ♔d6 65.♘c4+ ♔c7 66.c3 ♘e7 67.♔e5 ♘g6+ 68.♔f5 ♘e7+ 69.♔e6 ♘g6 70.a5 White has made minimal progress, and this last advance may be seen as a final push.

70...b5?

A curious error, especially in view of the fact that White now has several winning knight moves. Anand must have been very tired. With 70...bxa5 71.♔d5 ♘f4+ 72.♔xc5 ♘e2 73.♘d6 ♘c1 74.♘b5+ ♔b7 75.♘d4 ♔a6!, Black would have had little trouble holding the endgame.

71.♘e3 71.♘d6 and 71.♘b6 would also have sufficed for the win.

71...♘f4+ 72.♔e5 ♘e2 73.♘d5+ ♔c6 74.b4 ♘xc3 75.♘xc3 cxb4 76.♘e2 An important final finesse. Black resigned, because the white knight gets to b3.

In the final round, Carlsen needed only a draw against Giri to win the tournament. Playing as Black, he didn't get into trouble at any point, especially because Giri went for a tame line of the Sveshnikov, But when Carlsen was in a position to pounce, he failed to do so.

Anish Giri
Magnus Carlsen
Wijk aan Zee 2019 (13)

position after 19.♖xa4

White has not achieved anything, and after the next move he is forced to make a positional exchange sacrifice that yields just about enough compensation.

19...♗c6 20.♗e2

But not like this! Correct was 20.♖xa6 ♗b5 21.♗e2 ♗xa6 22.♗xa6 f5 23.exf5 ♖xf5 24.♗c4, with a solid blockade.

20...♗xa4 21.♕xa4 f5

White has just used up too much time and is unable to maintain the blockade correctly.

22.exf5 ♖xf5 23.♗d3 ♖f8 24.♕xa6

Wasting even more time. He should have taken with the bishop.

24...♗d2 25.♕c4

25...♕c8

Carlsen had 40 minutes left and played the text at once. Later he said that he had seen a drawing line and that he was happy with that result. This is very strange. Against Vidit he tried for nearly 100 moves to win a drawn endgame, whereas here he showed no ambition at all in a superior position. Then, in Round 3, Carlsen wanted to win at all cost, but now, as in his final match game against Caruana in London last autumn, he didn't seem to care.

About that draw last year, Dubov said in the previous issue: 'This is exactly the type of decision that makes one a World Champion.' All well and good, but Karpov and Kasparov, to mention just two of Carlsen's illustrious predecessors, would certainly have gone for the win in that position against Caruana, all the more so because a draw did not clinch the title. In addition, the two Ks were always trying to win tournaments in superior fashion.

With that much time on the clock, they would certainly have gone for 25...♖c8 26.♕e4 ♖c1! in the diagrammed position. Swapping rooks is very good for Black, since it will make it hard for White to defend f2. The opposite-coloured bishops guarantee Black a strong and decisive attack. The white passed pawns on the b-file are of little consequence. After 27.g3 ♕a8 28.b5 ♕a2, White will have little to hope for, so if Carlsen had made the effort, he could have won the tournament with a one-and-a-half point lead. But as Giri already observed during the game, the World Champion was in a hurry; in a hurry to win the tournament.

26.♕e4 ♗xb4 27.♘xb4 ♖f4 28.♕c6 ♖fxb4 29.♕xd6 ♕f8 30.♕xe5+

And here Giri offered a draw, again speculating that Carlsen was in a rush. He was right, because the offer was accepted almost immediately. Black, incidentally, no longer has realistic winning chances. ∎

Jorden van Foreest

CURRENT ELO: **2618**

DATE OF BIRTH: **April 30, 1999**

PLACE OF BIRTH: **Utrecht, the Netherlands**

PLACE OF RESIDENCE: **Groningen, the Netherlands**

What is your favourite city?
Groningen.

What was the last great meal you had?
Pizza with a friend of mine last night.

What drink brings a smile to your face?
Innocent Smoothies.

Which book would you give to a friend?
Flow: The Psychology of optimal experience by Mihaly Csikszentmihalyi.

What book is currently on your bedside table?
Never Split the Difference by Chris Voss.

What is your all-time favourite movie?
Inglourious Basterds.

And your favourite TV series?
Game of Thrones.

Do you have a favourite actor?
Leonardo DiCaprio.

And a favourite actress?
Emilia Clarke.

What music do you listen to?
Any genre, from rap to EDM.

Is there a work of art that moves you?
The Scream by Edvard Munch.

Who is your favourite chess player of all time?
Garry Kasparov; his play came with such strength and energy.

Is there a chess book that had a profound influence on you?
All of Kasparov's books on his matches vs Karpov.

What was your best result ever?
Becoming Dutch Champion in 2016.

And the best game you played?
My win against Duda from the 2019 Tata Steel Masters was quite good.

What was the most exciting chess game you ever saw?
Bai Jinshi-Ding Liren, 2017.

What is your favourite square?
c3.

Do chess players have typical shortcomings?
Their wardrobe.

What are chess players particularly good at (except for chess)?
Eloquence.

Do you have any superstitions?
I used to try and play with the same pen in case I won, but since I kept on losing my pens it didn't make much sense.

Facebook, Instagram, Snapchat, or?
Twitter @jordenvforeest.

How many friends do you have on Facebook?
586.

Who do you follow on Twitter?
Anish Giri.

What is your life motto?
Keep it simple, ask others.

When were you happiest?
In general, I am a happy person, but after winning the European Championship U14 in 2013 I was especially happy.

Who or what would you like to be if you weren't yourself?
An aerospace engineer.

Which three people would you like to invite for dinner?
Elon Musk, Magnus Carlsen and Radio Jan.

What is the best piece of advice you were ever given?
To try and become a professional chess player.

Is there something you'd love to learn?
How to juggle.

Where is your favourite place in the world?
On cloud nine.

What is your greatest fear?
Drowning.

And your greatest regret?
I started playing the Najdorf too late in my career.

If you could change one thing in the chess world, what would it be?
Anishilate the draw offer.

What does it mean to be a chess player?
Having a lot of freedom.

Is a knowledge of chess useful in everyday life?
I don't particularly think so.

What is the best thing that was ever said about chess?
Your chess style represents your personality.